Sailor in the Desert

The colour photographs in this book are of oil paintings by Phillip Gunn, now part of the British National Art Collection.

Sailor in the Desert

The Adventures of Phillip Gunn DSM, RN in the Mesopotamia Campaign 1915

David Gunn

Pen & Sword
MARITIME

First published in Great Britain in 2013 by
Pen & Sword Maritime
an imprint of
Pen & Sword Books Ltd
47 Church Street
Barnsley
South Yorkshire
S70 2AS

Copyright © David Gunn 2013

ISBN 978 1 78346 230 8

Typeset in Ehrhardt by
Mac Style, Driffield, East Yorkshire
Printed and bound in India by Replika Press Pvt. Ltd.

Pen & Sword Books Ltd incorporates the imprints of Pen & Sword
Archaeology, Atlas, Aviation, Battleground, Discovery,
Family History, History, Maritime, Military, Naval, Politics,
Railways, Select, Social History, Transport, True Crime,
and Claymore Press, Frontline Books, Leo Cooper, Praetorian Press,
Remember When, Seaforth Publishing and Wharncliffe.

For a complete list of Pen & Sword titles please contact
PEN & SWORD BOOKS LIMITED
47 Church Street, Barnsley, South Yorkshire, S70 2AS, England
E-mail: enquiries@pen-and-sword.co.uk
Website: www.pen-and-sword.co.uk

Contents

Maps

Acknowledgements

My thanks are due to Mary J. de Merindol, who helped me with the first draft of this book, and Abbie Ratcliffe, Publishing Manager at Imperial War Museums, who commented on the accuracy of the details, and for her wise guidance. I am also grateful to my extended family for their unwavering support.

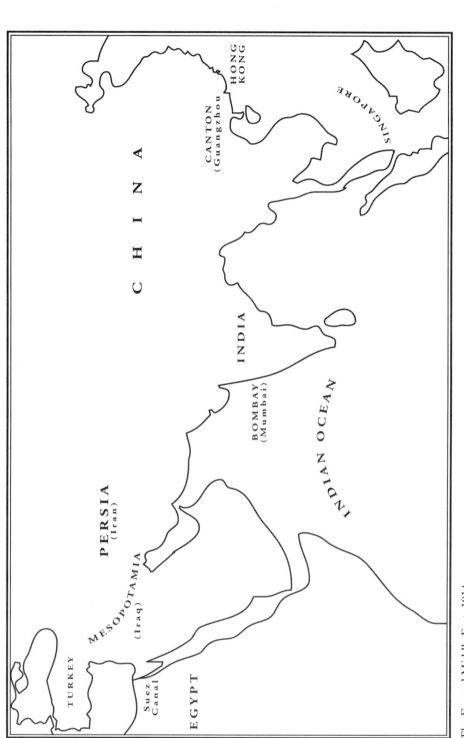

The Far and Middle East, 1914.

Chapter 1

A Shark Steals the Dinner

He should have seen the shadow of the shark as it slid menacingly through the turquoise South China Sea astern of His Majesty's Ship *Clio*, driven forward under her sails. But all he saw was the shark's head as it closed in on the bag he had been towing. It half-rolled to the right and seized the bag in its scimitar-shaped mouth; there was a violent shake, and the rope went limp.

Ordinary Seaman Phil Gunn dejectedly reeled the bag in. It had contained his mess's dinner. It was a leg of salt pork that the shark had got; trailing it in the sea, surprisingly, reduced the salt content of the meat. As cook-of-the-mess that day (see illustration) preparation of the midday dinner had been his responsibility and now he had lost it.

'What's up lad?' demanded Petty Officer Jock Bryce, who happened to be passing on the poop deck.

'A shark got the pork, PO,' explained Phil, helplessly regarding the frayed rope's end. As the ship had been mainly up the rivers of China he had not come across this problem before. 'The lads won't be happy.'

'I warned you about that,' said Bryce, who had also given the young seaman the tip about reducing the salt. 'You need to keep your eyes open for 'em at sea. Perhaps you'll listen next time. Get down to the galley. See if they've got any grub to spare.'

Meat had not been a problem when they left Hong Kong with a herd of cattle and some sheep on the upper deck. The Royal Marine butcher would kill one when required, the distressed beast being pulled unwillingly with ropes by the duty watch of seamen towards the upper deck scupper (see illustration). In the case of the cattle the animal would then be poleaxed with a sledgehammer. The carcase would be cut up, blood and offal running into the sea through the chute designed to keep the ship's side clean.

Phil didn't like the spectacle of the animals suffering but in 1913 there was no refrigeration in this class of ship. So the fresh meat was better than the salt pork they had to draw in barrels from the dockyard for longer voyages. Chances were that the same barrels had been issued to ships in previous commissions so the pork tended to be far from fresh.

The galley had some cold beef left over from yesterday. Phil served it up to his eight fellow seamen together with the potatoes and carrots he had prepared for their midday dinner. There were grumbles but, to his relief, also some laughs.

*   *   *

HMS *Clio*, a sloop (see illustration), was one of the last of the Royal Navy's sailing warships. As was often the custom in times of peace away from Britain, she had been painted a gleaming white enamel, with a black stripe around her sides. Her bows bore a figurehead in the form of a scantily clad lady surrounded by gold leaf scrollwork and her three tall wooden masts were immaculately scraped and varnished. Between the first and second masts a tall funnel sloped gently back at the same angle, for *Clio* had steam engines as well as sails.

On seeing her for the first time, Phil had thought she looked more like the magnificent steam yacht of a rich oriental gentleman but *Clio* also packed a punch. In and around the decks were six 4-inch calibre guns, which could hit hard and accurately, the 4-inch measurement indicating the diameter of the shells they fired. There was also some smaller armament.

She was on her way north in December 1913 to return to the waterway that led from the British port of Hong Kong up to Canton. There she would resume her normal task of patrolling the rivers of Southern China in support of a large number of British traders.

The captain had decided they would use sails for the voyage to Hong Kong. The square sails on her foremast, much like those of the ships that had won the Battle of Trafalgar, had recently been discontinued as part of the Royal Navy's move towards steam. However, fore and aft sails, as might be seen in yachts at the Cowes Regatta, bore the 10-year-old sloop economically along. From time to time, day and night, came the shrill, haunting whistle of the bosun's pipe and call to the duty watch of seamen to adjust the set of the sails. This would be for a change of wind direction or alteration of the ship's course.

On eventual arrival at Canton they found vessels from other countries and both sailors and officers of *Clio* were glad to see their friends in a German cruiser, His Majesty's Ship *Emden*. In *Emden*'s case it was a different 'Majesty' from King George V in the form of his cousin, Kaiser Wilhelm II. After the normal church parade on Sundays sailors from each ship manned and rowed boats across to visit the other. On Christmas Day 1913 it was estimated that there were more of *Emden*'s men in *Clio* than their own, and vice versa. On Boxing Day, *Emden*'s ship's company gave a concert in a theatre ashore to entertain the British sailors. They created a backdrop of the *Clio* and good-heartedly mimicked British naval habits and customs.

Chapter 2

The International Arms Race

Phillip Gunn (see illustration) had joined the Royal Navy as a boy seaman in 1911. He started this hard life at the bottom just as his father and grandfather had, having failed the exams that would have enabled him to start halfway up as an officer. It wasn't that he was stupid, but his father's naval postings had been such that he was never at the same school long enough for a coherent education. Father had blamed Phil's failure on his love of football but Phil didn't mind and revelled in the life he now led.

Britain was enjoying a century of predominant peace, but there were murmurings of unease. Germany, Austria and Russia, all with European empires, felt threatened by large minorities who wanted greater democracy. Germany, an expanding power, also felt encircled by Russia, France and Britain in a way that hindered its trade and development as a nation. It was also ruled by a paranoid kaiser. France and Britain were in a different category. They both controlled vast overseas empires, of which their European neighbours were jealous.

Germany in particular resented its lack of colonies and was embarking on doing something about it. A race to build a fleet to rival the Royal Navy's supremacy at sea had been running since 1900. This was matched by the British, who had developed a superior type of battleship known as dreadnoughts, and they were also involved in this arms race. 'We want eight [dreadnoughts] and we won't wait!' was a cry from the British population that had gone up across the country. It was proud of its empire but had been made aware of potential threats from Germany in particular. On land Germany and France were rapidly expanding their armies but Britain, an island nation with a far-flung empire, relied on the power of a large navy. Nobody had argued much with this since the Battle of Trafalgar in 1805.

On the extremities of Europe, Germany had forged good relations with Turkey. The former saw this as a way of gaining access to the Middle East and eventually threatening Britain's dominance of the Persian Gulf and India.

But such matters did not affect relations between the ships' companies of *Clio* and *Emden* and were unlikely to be of interest to a teenage seaman. Phil's daily concerns were more likely to be scrubbing the decks, pushing the capstan bars round to raise the anchor, manning the sails or being lowered and hoisted in a seaboat.

After a few months of cruising the China rivers, having passed the necessary exams, Phil had been advanced to ordinary seaman. 'You can smoke now,' Petty Officer Bryce had told him. 'Go to the canteen and get yourself a pipe.' Phil did as he was told, buying himself a clay pipe for a penny. Jock Bryce handed him his tobacco pouch, from which the boy filled the pipe, lit up and began to puff in a rather uncertain way. After five uncomfortable minutes he had turned green, rushed to the heads[1] and was sick. The brutal navy leaf tobacco had been too much for him.

Phil took gradually to smoking a pipe, as did many of his fellow seamen. It was a badge of experience and he began to find it strangely soothing, especially when keeping watch in cold weather on deck or as a lookout.

He liked his fellow seamen. Most were from far rougher backgrounds than his and he was sometimes referred to as 'a bit of a toff'. This was because he spoke in a more precise manner than most, but it was said jovially and without malice. Being forced to work up masts (see illustration), in seaboats and around the capstan and to live together naturally moulded most into good messmates. There was inevitably the odd bully but Phil was large and confident enough and did not suffer from this.

As soon as he was eligible Phil took the examinations for able seaman. He would not be 'rated up' to an AB until the requisite time had elapsed but at least he was now qualified for it.

Up the rivers *Clio* steamed continuously, often in the intense heat of the South China summer. Even the trained stokers were collapsing as they shovelled coal into the boilers. Seamen from the upper deck were called upon to give relief and for a week Phil found himself down in the stokehold of the ship with a shovel in his hand. He and his fellow seamen gasped for breath as the furnace doors were opened and an intense red heat sprang out at them as they shovelled their coal into the fiery inferno (see illustration). He gained considerable respect for a stoker's work in a coal-burning ship.

Note

1. Lavatory.

Chapter 3

A Seaman's Work – Early 1914

Following a few days back in Hong Kong *Clio* sailed for a new task. Charts of the coast of Borneo urgently needed improvement but the specially fitted-out surveying ship was undergoing repairs. The sloop, little more than a sailing ship with modern guns and no specialist equipment, took her place.

Clio anchored in a bay for the night and the following morning surveying parties were detailed off. Phil was in one led by the ship's second-in-command, Lieutenant Commander Edgar Cookson.

'Come on. Chop chop!' urged Cookson as his team of seamen lowered the cutter from its davits into the water and passed down the surveying equipment. They clambered down ropes and started to row inshore but the water was too shallow to get right in. Phil volunteered to hop over the side and was laden with the theodolite, balls of spun yarn, axes and other equipment they would need. He began to wade ashore, initially part supported by the water but as it got shallower his feet started to sink into the seabed. He found it increasingly difficult to drag one foot in front of the other. Eventually he could not lift his feet at all and was slowly sinking down into the mud.

Suddenly frightened, he shouted across the 40 yards that separated him from Cookson, who was now ashore.

'I can't move Sir!'

The officer turned to take in the situation. Back came a crisp order to Phil to let himself fall forward onto the mud and wriggle ashore. He did so and, gently encouraged by Cookson, to his profound relief found his legs and feet slowly pulling up out of the enveloping quagmire as he eased himself forward to the beach. It didn't cross his mind to discard the heavy equipment that was dragging him down, which surprised him when he thought about it later.

Cookson took him by the arm, still covered in the slime of the bay, to rest against the trunk of a tree. In its welcome shade he sat down and talked to

Phil, asking the young man about his life at home, his interests and gently reviving his shaken spirits. Phil was normally used to barked orders from the *Clio's* second-in-command, who worked the ship's company hard. But he was aware that this tough officer was also prepared to make one with the sailors in the football team although, like most officers, his game was really rugby. Phil discovered a degree of sympathy and understanding of which he had not previously been aware.

Over the next few weeks they checked and amended the charts of the area, erected leading marks on the shore and measured the depths – work that was too complex for Phil as an ordinary seaman to fully understand. At the end of each day they rowed back to the ship, sometimes as much as 5 miles, tired and sunburned.

Lack of specialist equipment meant that surveying in the old sloop was some of the toughest physical work *Clio's* ship's company had undertaken. Apart from landing to survey and carry out sounding, it was necessary to anchor the ship as many as eight times a day. As she had no power appliances when it came to weighing anchor, sixteen seamen were needed each time, pushing with their chests on the wooden bars round the capstan (see illustration).

* * *

The business of surveying involved the constant lowering and hoisting of boats, which were suspended on ropes at both bow and stern. On one occasion when his surveying party returned to the ship, Phil was required to remain at one end of the boat and steady the block through which the hoisting rope was passing. He made the error of holding onto the rope itself only to see his fingers drawn into the iron wheel of the block through which it passed and on which the 2-ton boat was hanging.

The officer in charge on board saw his plight and immediately shouted, 'Avast[1] hauling!'

Shocked and bewildered, Phil could only utter, 'Yessir! 'vast hauling.' The boat was lowered a little. His fingers, to his horror, apparently mangled flesh and blood, came out of the block. He was helped out of the boat and taken to the ship's sick bay. Phil felt faint but didn't lose consciousness. Numbed as he was, he felt no pain, even as the ship's surgeon lifted off a fingernail hanging on only by its corner.

Phil did not lose the use of any fingers, but was to bear the scars and some awkward fingernails permanently. It was some compensation that shortly afterwards he was promoted to able seaman.

In addition to the landing of surveying parties, *Clio* had to carry out depth sounding offshore. To do this the navigating officer kept an exact check of her position by taking bearings off the land as she steamed along. Soundings of the depth of the water were then taken to chart this accurately.

Unlike most naval ships of the day the old sloop had no special fittings for this work. Phil, or one of his shipmates, merely stood in one of the boats slung out from the side of the ship. They would heave a 12-pound lead weight on a rope round in a great circle, releasing it horizontally in the direction in which the ship was travelling. The lead flew forward, dropping into the sea and down to the seabed. The leadsman, as he was known, would then reel in the line and as it became vertical with the ship's forward movement note the mark on the rope, which indicated the depth of the water. He would shout up to the bridge 'By the mark 6' if, say, the 6 fathom[2] mark showed at the surface.

Not only was a two-hour 'trick' as leadsman arduous work but Phil had only recently lacerated his fingertips in the hoisting block. One particularly cold day increased the pain in his fingers until it became agony and after a while he appealed to Petty Officer Bryce to be relieved. Bryce would have none of it and made him finish his trick. This became the only occasion Phil felt he was subjected to unreasonable hardship in the *Clio*.

Notes

1. Stop.
2. A fathom is 6 feet or 1.83 metres.

Chapter 4

War

Charting completed, the captain ordered a course for Singapore to refuel.

Coaling ship meant the embarkation of many tons. Everyone took part – sailors, stokers, officers and others – which had the positive effect of uniting the ship's company in this dirty task. Only the telegraphists, whose fingers needed the sensitivity to tap out morse on the new wireless equipment, as well as the bandsmen and the padre, were excused.

They got into their oldest clothes. Tugs came up towing steel barges full of coal, which were secured alongside. Filthy task that it was, Phil enjoyed its competitive nature as each part of ship – forecastle, maintop, foretop and quarterdeck – tried to defeat the others in the speed with which it emptied its particular barge. Taking up a heavy shovel Phil jumped down into his barge. He sought shelter in one of the corners while large, stiff sacks were hurled down from the upper deck to be filled with coal as rapidly as possible (see illustration). From a derrick on the upper deck was lowered a rope with a hook on its end. In succession this would be taken to the four corners of the barge for filled bags to be hooked onto and hoisted up by a team of seamen. They would then manoeuvre the sacks and empty them down into the circular holes that led to the coal hold. As the level of coal in the lighter fell, Phil and others found themselves working down into the corners, sweating in the tropical heat. Coal dust rose everywhere into the air like a black, dense fog and suddenly he found himself short of breath.

'PO, it's getting down my throat and I can't breathe!' he called to Petty Officer Bryce on the upper deck.

'Well shove a knob of coal in your mouth, you young fathead; that will keep it shut.'

Sure enough, it did the trick.

* * *

One day as July 1914 gave way to August, the captain of HMS *Clio* called all hands on deck. His message was sombre.

He told the ship's company that Great Britain had just declared war on Germany, news that caused a stirring in the assembled ranks of sailors. He pointed out that this had been brewing for some time, that Germany had invaded Belgium in order to attack France and that Britain had joined France and Russia in defence of Belgium.

The captain then went on to explain how all this might affect them in the *Clio*. Germany had a number of warships here in the Far East and these would be trying to sink British merchant shipping. He reminded them that many of them had German friends in the cruiser *Emden* whom they used to meet on rivers in China and at Canton. It was now *Clio's* job to seek out and attempt to sink her and any other German warships they found.

More than a few of the *Clio* ship's company wondered how they, with their six guns firing 4-inch diameter shells, were going to sink the *Emden*, which had ten guns of similar calibre and was faster. However, a sister ship and some torpedo boats were to accompany them.

The duty cook of the mess would prepare the meals, take them to the galley to be cooked, and serve them up on the mess table. Results were variable. (*Sketch by Phillip Gunn. Copyright, the author*)

They prepared for war. Among the preparations was the need to obliterate the gleaming white of the ship's side and make *Clio* less conspicuous. As was frequently the custom in the Royal Navy, *Clio's* second-in-command, Lieutenant Commander Cookson, had paid for the ornate decoration out of his own pocket. With much sadness they were now obliged to cover it, the gilded scrolls on bow and stern and the highly varnished wooden masts with dull grey paint. Cookson was forced to look on in acceptance of its necessity.

In Singapore the war in Europe seemed far away, almost belonging to a different world. However, as men of a fighting service, the sailors were regarded as heroic by the local British population despite the fact that they had done no fighting. Entertainment of all kinds was laid on for them.

In order to keep the ship's company fit, early morning route marches were ordered, some 8 miles to and from a military barracks. The sailors bore heavy rifles but Phil had a slight musical talent that stood him in good stead. His role was to carry and play an infinitely lighter fife as a member of the drum and fife band that accompanied the marches (see illustration).

Clio was ordered once again to the waters around Borneo, where it was suspected the *Emden* was lying in wait for British merchant shipping. The British ship's captain and Captain von Muller of the *Emden* had developed a close friendship in China. Now, every other day *Clio* would receive over her wireless telegraphy equipment a strange but friendly signal giving *Emden's* position: but it was her position as it had been two or three days earlier and was always accompanied by a humorous greeting. *Clio's* captain kept his ship's company informed of these signals. Phil found it hard to reconcile them and the jovial associations he had enjoyed with the German sailors at Canton with the generally held British supposition that Germans had no sense of humour. It also helped him to understand that whereas it was the fighting sailor's job to kill his enemy, you didn't have to hate him while doing so.

They saw nothing of the *Emden* or any other enemy vessels. With the peace of the tropical seas about them it seemed strange to think that Britain was involved in a devastating war on the other side of the world.

Chapter 5

The Navy's Fuel Supply is Threatened

Mr Winston Churchill, First Lord of the Admiralty since 1911, had much on his mind. It was September 1914 and likely that Turkey would join Germany in its war against Britain, Russia and France. Turkey had a potential stranglehold over access to the oilfield in South Persia (now Iran), from which much of the Royal Navy's fuel oil came. It flowed through a pipeline to Abadan on the Persian shore of the Shatt al Arab estuary, from where oil tankers took it away. Troubling Churchill's mind must have been that the other side of the Shatt was Mesopotamia (now Iraq), which the Turkish Ottoman Empire had ruled for some 400 years.

Should they have switched over from coal? Churchill had actively encouraged the move to oil and the modern ships of the fleet were much better for it … provided you could get the stuff. Britain also needed to show a strong presence in the Persian Gulf, where it had influential, but less robust allies. It was totally committed elsewhere in its struggle against the Germans so it would be the government in India that would have to send troops to protect the oil supplies.

However, there was one thing the Admiralty could do. Signals were sent to two sloops, of the same class as HMS *Clio*, to proceed to the Shatt al Arab waterway. Their presence would have an impact there but they would also be able to provide gunfire support with their 4-inch guns to the troops that India may well have to send. The sloops were of shallow draught, which was important as they could negotiate the shoaling rivers of Mesopotamia. They would be able to patrol the waterways between Persia and that land to protect British oil interests.

Subsequently, *Clio* was also ordered to break away from the pursuit of their old friend the *Emden*[1] and proceed to the Persian Gulf. She headed across the Indian Ocean, a barrel strapped to the top of the foremast (see illustration) from which a lookout could warn of the possible approach of German warships. These were harassing and indeed sinking British merchant shipping. Phil was frequently given lookout duty and found it extremely uncomfortable to stand with his 6-foot body in the barrel. So he sat on its rim, leaving his feet dangling outside, and sang all the songs he knew to offset the discomfort.

When the ship pitched he would sometimes see the cocked-up bowsprit in front of him plunge under the waves ahead. Would it ever come up again or were they headed for the bottom? When she rolled, the long yardarm out to the side of the foremast would similarly dip into the waves on the beam. But the ship constructors had done their job well and the ship's officers knew what they were doing. *Clio* kept going.

Note

1. Having caused considerable damage to British merchant shipping, *Emden* was eventually destroyed by His Majesty's Australian Ship *Sydney* at the Cocos Keeling Islands in November 1914.

Chapter 6

Turks Attack the Suez Canal

Before *Clio* could get to the Persian Gulf another situation emerged. The Turks were seen to be advancing down through Syria and Palestine towards the Suez Canal. If they were allowed to stop traffic through the canal essential supplies to the Allies' war effort in Europe would be cut off; so would the ships bringing vital troops from India and Australasia.

Clio was accordingly diverted to Suez. This was halfway to Britain and her crew were due to be replaced by a relief crew that they knew had already sailed from England. So hopes were high – particularly among the married men – for a return home, even if that meant going back to a much more intensive war zone.

On arrival at the canal it became evident that the sloop was to join a number of British and French warships lining it as floating fortresses to keep the Turkish Army at bay. Initially *Clio* was sent up to moor at Port Said, where Egyptians offering goods for sale surrounded her in small boats. From past experience, the Egyptians had found that soldiers and sailors were particularly gullible purchasers of fancy items to take home. Men in flowing robes came aboard to give magic shows, which involved producing day-old chicks from most unexpected parts of their clothing. They accompanied this by saying '*Gully-gully*', and were accordingly known as gully-gully men.

One boat displayed exotic-looking stringed instruments that were, in fact, mandolins. To add to his sales pitch the vendor lolled back in his craft, smiling broadly, while playing catchy tunes of the time that he knew would appeal to the men. It sounded great. It looked easy. Phil was among six sailors who purchased one. They then found that such a bulky item was difficult to stow in the very limited confines of a sloop's messdeck. Somehow they stuffed them in above the piping that ran under the deck above their mess.

It had been implied by the vendor that anyone could play a mandolin but after a few weeks there remained on board only that one possessed by Phil. He was the sole owner with any pretension of musical ability and managed to knock out a few tunes, which was better, but only just better, than no music at all. It would be one more item to add to the sailor's luggage of a kitbag, hammock, cap box, ditty box[1] and straw hat cover. But on returning from a foreign commission sailors also wanted to bring home souvenirs for their loved ones. There would be the parrot or canary in a cage, china tea set or leather pouffe cover. Phil would have his mandolin.

They were not long at Port Said as the Turkish Army was advancing from the east across the inhospitable Sinai Desert towards the canal. *Clio* was ordered to take up a position at Al Qantara. Other ships were moored at different points, their guns trained towards the desert. Contingents of soldiers were stationed on the banks ready to repel any attempted Turkish incursion. Cavalry scouting parties went out into the desert to reconnoitre enemy troop movements.

During daylight hours movements were evident on the desert horizon. Phil could also see the flashes of distant Turkish field guns aiming at the masts of the ships, including those of *Clio*, along the canal. After a flash you knew that a shell would shortly land nearby. You hoped it would not be on your ship, or even on you. This was the first time that Phil had been involved in real enemy action. He found it frightening yet exhilarating. As the ships were penned in the canal it was not difficult for the Turks to find the range of them and shells fell all around *Clio*. It became necessary to warp her from one bank of the canal to the other from time to time to spoil the gunners' aim and avoid the fall of shot.

One day Phil was on the bridge during a warping operation when a shrapnel bullet burst immediately overhead, throwing small pieces of metal in all directions. It did little harm other than remove the Egyptian pilot's straw boater, which the pilot subsequently kept as a souvenir, proudly displaying the shrapnel hole.

As twilight approached, lookouts at the mastheads closely scanned the middle and foregrounds. They kept especially close watch on the sparse tufts of desert vegetation near the canal but never a sign of life appeared. Nevertheless, without fail, as soon as darkness fell concealed snipers from the canal bank would commence to fire their rifles. They appeared to aim mainly at the ship's searchlights, which were endeavouring to both seek out the snipers and spot any general Turkish advance at night.

Sandbags were placed around the vulnerable parts of the upper deck to safeguard the ship's company as they went about their duties.

One night, Phil was part of a body of sailors detailed off to land in a boat on the west bank, away from the Turks. Their task was to secure a wire hawser to a bollard on the shore, the other end of the wire then to be taken to the capstan on *Clio's* forecastle. This would be turned by a team of his shipmates to reel in the wire and haul the ship across the canal, making the Turkish gunners' aim more difficult.

As Phil stumbled up the bank towards the bollard in the pitch darkness, there was suddenly a blinding flash followed by a rifle shot close at hand. His heart appeared to stop as he wondered where he had been hit and why he was still standing. It seemed an age before he realized that the flash had been the ship's searchlight beam reflecting off the white bollard as it swung around in an arc. The shot? Possibly the sound of a sniper's shot from the other side of the canal reflected off a nearby surface in the otherwise silent night. He never found out.

Clio had embarked a military observing officer to direct her guns in support of the army. Sometimes when Turkish troops were sighted and in range, the ship was called upon to bombard them and deter any advance towards the Suez Canal.

On one occasion they were enthusiastically firing across the desert at distant troop movements. The enemy had not replied. Suddenly an army officer on horseback was seen galloping fast along the eastern canal bank towards the ship, which was moored on the other side. He came to a halt and shouted across to *Clio*. Not only was he some distance away but also out of breath from his rapid ride. They could not hear what he was saying and so went on with their bombardment.

Eventually he got his breath back and the message across. *Clio* was bombarding one of the British Army's own scouting parties that had been sent out from headquarters further along the canal. Nobody quite worked out whose fault it was.

The Turks' major attack on the Suez Canal came at night on 3 February 1915. They advanced in strength with troops and artillery towards a point halfway down the canal some distance south of *Clio*. Meeting stiff opposition they managed to get three boatloads of troops across the canal, all of whom were killed, wounded or captured.

Following this failure the Turks retreated to concentrate their military efforts in Mesopotamia. The vital sea route through Suez was safe, at least for now.

Note

1. Container for personal possessions.

Chapter 7

A Brief Refit in Bombay

Clio's ship's company had now been away from home for three years. The Admiralty's plan had been for it to be replaced by another crew, which had sailed from England some time previously. However, news now came that the reliefs, having reached Malta, had been turned back. The disappointment for Phil was less than for those who had wives and families awaiting their return. It was due to 'the exigencies of the service in wartime', explained *Clio's* captain.

It was for the Persian Gulf and Mesopotamia that she now sailed.

First of all there was to be a short refit in Bombay (now Mumbai), which was then a port with comprehensive facilities for the Royal Navy. They arrived to find the weather unexpectedly humid. The Great Monsoon that normally arrives from the south-west in June, transporting moisture-laden air from the Indian Ocean, had put out its feelers at a different time of year. Bombay was unpleasantly hot and damp, especially so in a steel ship down in a dry dock away from the cooling effect of the sea. Accordingly it was decided that the ship's company would sleep in the 'Sailors' Home' in the city. They would march to and from the ship each day. Many soldiers were also accommodated there.

So heavy was the tropical rain that the sailors' clothing was totally inadequate against it. In due course a consignment of umbrellas arrived at the home for added protection. This resulted in the bizarre spectacle of 150 sailors marching in columns of four through the streets of the city, each carrying an umbrella. It provided a matchless target for the humour of the soldiers watching them from the windows, the ribald comments of whom caused great discomfiture to their nautical colleagues.

It was necessary for a small number of men to remain close to the ship at night to deal with any emergency that might arise. As *Clio* was too hot to sleep in, the duty sailors slung their hammocks under the roofs of the open-sided sheds on the dockside.

One night, as one of the duty watch, Phil slept badly. He had been feeling unwell in this alien climate and was brusquely woken in the morning with the unwelcome information that he was 'on the carpet' – in trouble. Apparently a typhoon had sprung up in the middle of the night, the duty watch of the hands had been called to go and secure the ship against the wind and rain and he had slept through it all. He had thus been absent from his place of duty and was arraigned before the ship's second-in-command as a defaulter the next day. Phil's excuse was deemed unacceptable and Lieutenant Commander Cookson awarded him a punishment involving extra work in the evenings for a few days.

While experiencing a certain feeling of personal shame, Phil took no umbrage. It seemed hard but he knew that a ship only functioned efficiently when every man could be relied on to do whatever authority required of him.

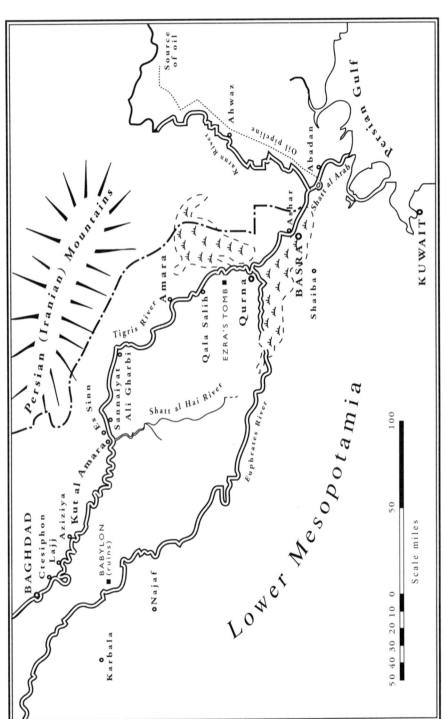

Lower Mesopotamia.

Chapter 8

HMS *Clio's* Role in Mesopotamia

From Bombay, *Clio* proceeded across the Arabian Sea heading for the Persian Gulf and the war against the Turks in Mesopotamia.

The army would be short of artillery so the navy would need to supply it. This would be possible as any military activity was likely to take place close to the rivers, the only source of fresh water for both cavalry horses and men. The captain ordered gunnery exercises, firing at floating objects in the sea to improve accuracy. He cleared the lower deck and explained the reason the ship was going to the Persian Gulf.

The Royal Navy was turning over to oil, rather than the coal *Clio* used in addition to her sails, the captain pointed out. Most of that oil came from southern Persia in a pipe to a place called Abadan, about 30 miles up the Shatt al Arab estuary.

Whereas the northern side of that estuary belonged to Persia, he went on, the southern side was Mesopotamia. This was a country of Arab tribes but ruled by the Turks, upon whom Britain had just declared war. It had been brewing for some time but the last straw was them bombarding a port in the Black Sea belonging to Britain's allies, the Russians. Another factor was that the Turks had been stirred up by the Germans, with whom Britain was at war, to have a go at the British Empire.

The captain went on to explain that *Clio's* role would be principally to support the army with her main armament of 4-inch guns. He had no doubt they would be called upon to fulfil other tasks as well. But the main reason they were going up the Persian Gulf was to protect Britain's oil supplies. He asked if there were any questions.

A leading seaman asked if there would be any shore leave.

When the opportunity arose, answered the captain, but he pointed out that they shouldn't expect there to be anything like Portsmouth, Malta or Hong Kong. He concluded by adding that they should be prepared for the climate to vary from extreme cold at night to boiling hot in the summer days. Every man should look after his health as a matter of priority.

* * *

The Shatt al Arab is the estuary of the two great rivers, Tigris and Euphrates. They each flow for more than 1,000 miles from Turkey to the sea through the land then known as Mesopotamia – the Ancient Greek word for 'land between rivers'. Prior to HMS *Clio* reaching the Shatt, some 4,000 British and Indian troops, led mostly by British officers, had come from India and landed there. They had driven the Turkish Army back through Basra, some 60 miles up from the sea, and away from the oil wells of southern Persia. What eventually became known as the Indian Expeditionary Force (IEF) had then been significantly increased in size. In company with two other Royal Navy sloops it had pushed on another 50 miles to capture Qurna, at the confluence of the two great rivers. A major victory over the Turks, who had been trying to retake Basra, had also been won to the west of that city at Shaiba. Before *Clio* had arrived there had been fierce fighting, with losses principally on the side of the Turks and Arab irregulars who supported them. The IEF had won some outstanding victories.

A debate then took place among the politicians and senior military men concerning what the IEF might do in Mesopotamia other than protect the oil supplies.

Chapter 9

The Politics

Mesopotamia came under the sphere of influence of British India as far as Britain was concerned. Lord Hardinge, Viceroy of India, had already sent tens of thousands of troops to the trenches in France and other theatres of war with the loyal and willing backing of the Indian people. He had done this with some trepidation as he had previously been forced to reduce the size of the Indian Army for financial reasons. The absence of these troops reduced India's ability to defend its own borders, and with Turkey a leading Muslim country there could be internal trouble from his own Muslim subjects. Hardinge had misgivings about the fact that the Indian Army was also now being asked to protect the Royal Navy's oil supplies as well as possibly embarking on other hostilities in the Middle East.

In the previous November, in 1914, Sir Percy Cox, Britain's Political Resident in the Persian Gulf, had seen things differently. He had telegraphed to the viceroy urging an advance, not only to safeguard Britain's oil supplies but also with the long-term aim of continuing and capturing Baghdad, the capital of Turkish-ruled Mesopotamia. His argument was that the defeat of the Turks to date had been so successful they were now terrified. They should be kept on the run and not allowed to regroup and threaten the IEF. The capture of Baghdad would also add to Britain's prestige throughout the Middle East and hopefully bring more people in on its side.

Cox felt that leaving the Turks in possession of Baghdad would give them a base from which to mount attacks on the British, now established in the south to protect the oil. The British capture of Basra had not only thrown the Turks into military disarray and therefore made them less able to resist an advance, it had also impressed the Arabs in the area that the invaders meant business and were worth siding with. However, if the IEF progressed no farther than Basra, it was Cox's contention that the Turks in Mesopotamia would be given time to recover.

Sir Percy Cox, pronounced by the Arabs as 'Supposi Kokus', also knew the mentality of the tribes along the Tigris and Euphrates. When you were winning they supported you; when you were losing they would try to exploit it to your disadvantage.

There was also the matter of climatic conditions. It was then the cool season, which would be good for campaigning across the normally inhospitable desert plains of Southern Mesopotamia. When March came, although the weather would be pleasant, the snow on the mountains of the Caucasus would start to melt and the whole area would gradually become one vast inland sea. Cox thought the IEF should get on.

Although not originally contemplated, such had been the success of the Mesopotamia campaign so far that a few politicians in London also started to regard the occupation of Baghdad as desirable.

With reservations, the Viceroy of India, Lord Hardinge, submitted the proposal to advance on Baghdad to the Secretary of State for India in London. The decision would have to be made by the British Government. The matter received short shrift. Baghdad lay some 570 miles from the sea up the river Tigris. It was along this waterway that our forces would need to be supplied – a dangerously long line of communication through a country whose inhabitants had no reason to be friendly. If the worst happened and a retreat from Baghdad became necessary, this would be disastrous for the British reputation in the Middle East. As far as Whitehall was concerned the object of the Mesopotamia expedition had been achieved. The oil supply for the Royal Navy was now safe, a strong British presence had been established in the Gulf and there was no point in attempting further territorial advances. The general commanding the troops was told to consolidate at Basra.

Chapter 10

The Aim Surreptitiously Changes

Whitehall also knew that, long term, a policy of inactivity was to be avoided for Britain to impress both Arabs and Indians with its ability to defeat any who defied it. It had therefore authorized the taking of the town of Qurna and this had happened. There the water was deep enough for armed sloops such as the *Clio*, now heading towards the Shatt. This depth varied with the time of year and according to how much meltwater was coming from the snows of the Caucasus into the river higher up.

In the House of Lords on 6 January 1915, the Secretary of State for War, Earl Kitchener of Khartoum, reported: 'In Mesopotamia our Indian Expeditionary Force has continued its northern advance from Basra and attacked the enemy at Qurna on the river Tigris, defeating the Turkish troops, inflicting heavy loss and capturing prisoners and guns. Since then the troops have consolidated the positions taken and have been warmly welcomed by the Arabs of the surrounding districts.'

In the same debate the Marquess of Crewe, Secretary of State for India, pointed out that 'This is a campaign for which the government of India are responsible. We are holding, as my noble and gallant friend pointed out, in some strength, the advance post of Qurna. We are not, at present, making anything like a general advance into Mesopotamia.'

Apart from the capture of Qurna the general in command of the army in Mesopotamia had been ordered to make his main base at Basra, and this he had done. However, in the spring of 1915 he fell ill and a new player took over.

General Sir John Nixon had been in command of the troops in North India. A fiery little cavalryman who enjoyed polo and pig sticking, he had a reputation for dash and enthusiasm. Before leaving India, Nixon had been given instructions that differed from those intended by Whitehall. Instead of primarily safeguarding the oil supplies for the Royal Navy, the IEF was firstly to retain complete control of Southern Mesopotamia. Securing the safety of the oil was now to be only of secondary importance.

Finally he was to submit a plan for a subsequent advance on Baghdad.

Chapter 11

Phil Meets the Arabs

As HMS *Clio* steamed up towards Basra in February 1915, Phil looked out onto Arab villages of large reed huts on the edge of marshland, with their goats and chickens around them. Water buffaloes, up to their necks in mud at the edge of the estuary, eased slowly out of the water as the warship approached. Phil was familiar with them having seen their like drawing ploughs through the rice paddies of China. Enclosures of reeds that rose vertically out of the water indicated the presence of fish traps.

The adult men, who regarded themselves as part of their tribe rather than of any nation, looked sullen. This was just another invading force intending to take over from the Turks, whose Ottoman Empire had controlled them with considerable difficulty for 400 years. In fact, the Turks had never really managed to control these Marsh Arabs, some of whom could be seen paddling their long, graceful canoes of planks covered in pitch as they went about their daily activities. The children waved as children the world over wave to a newcomer.

There was shore leave. Phil walked into Basra's little port town of Ashar and wandered around the bazaar with his friend Archie, both in their clean white sailors' suits and straw hats. They looked at the material, spices, sweet cakes and stalls selling ornaments that they were not sophisticated enough to realize would look incongruous if brought back to a western home. They stopped to sit and drink strong, sweet coffee at a street café.

A young Arab, better dressed in a clean white robe than most of the streetgoers, glanced at them curiously from an adjacent table and looked away. In due course he looked again, leant across and, speaking heavily accented English, asked if they would mind him talking to them. They consented and he came to sit at their table.

'Where do you live, Abdul?' asked Archie.

'My name is not Abdul. It is Mohammed, and I live on the edge of the town,' replied the Arab. 'I spoke English classes at the British Consulate. That's why I know English.'

'What do you think about us being here?' enquired Phil.

Mohammed shrugged. 'The Turks have ruled us for hundreds of years. They want a country called Mesopotamia and to make money out of us. We just want to live in our tribes as we have for thousands of years. We expect you will be the same as the Turks.'

'So you don't mind who runs Mesopotamia?'

'The people here just want to be left alone. If we have to take sides we join the side that is winning. We fight against the side that is losing. And we make as much out of it as we can from whoever interferes with us.'

This was a new idea to the young seamen who had been brought up to believe that the British were welcome everywhere. Phil asked the Arab where his family came from.

'They are in Amara, 100 miles up the river Tigris,' explained Mohammed. 'Your ship would be too big to get that far up the river but shallower boats can.'

He asked them some questions about their own home life and said he would like to go to England at some time but doubted he ever would. Politely he excused himself, rose and walked off up the sandy street.

They paid for their coffee and wandered on through the market. It was good to be off the ship after such a long time at sea. Arab traders manning the stalls treated them with respect but also with restraint. The British-led IEF had pushed their Turkish masters out of the Basra area. However, if they returned, the Turks, with a reputation for ruthless brutality, would give short shrift to anyone known to have fraternized with their enemy. And there were plenty of potential informers about.

They paused at a stall selling brass and copper goods. Phil enquired the price of a coffee pot that he thought his mother might like and pulled some coins out of the pocket of his bell-bottomed trousers to count them. Then Archie and he worked out that on 1s 7d (8p) a day that would be a week's pay, so he put his money away and they wandered on.

Later that evening and back on board, Phil remembered the case he had bought for his mother in Hong Kong. It opened out on hinges in the middle to reveal two glass-fronted displays of beautiful butterflies. It had cost him a month's pay but had fallen onto the deck and smashed during a storm off Japan.

Phil occasionally had thoughts of the rest of the family, wondering how they all were back at 209 Kingston Road, Teddington. They had always rented houses before because Father, a retired Royal Navy chief gunner, had moved around as the navy demanded. But Phil could recall overhearing conversations that they were buying a house this time. It would cost £250 and his father would have to take out a considerable mortgage to afford it. He didn't really know what a mortgage was but gathered it involved borrowing money that would have to be paid back some day. Then there was elder sister Ida, now working in domestic service, and younger brother Sydney at school. Thinking of them all seemed to bring him closer to home. It brought a slight lump into his throat when he did so but was nevertheless comforting.

Chapter 12

The Disgusting Garden of Eden

After a few days at Basra to coal ship and replenish, *Clio* slipped from her mooring buoys and headed north up the Shatt al Arab to join the forces at Qurna. *Clio's* sister ships *Espiegle* and *Odin* were already there. The weather was getting hotter.

Once again the captain addressed the ship's company. Qurna was said to be the original site of the Garden of Eden, he explained, going on to point out that he didn't think there would be much of interest for those going on shore leave there but that they should take care. He explained that the people here were theoretically neutral and we had no argument with them, but there would probably be spies in Turkish pay in amongst the Arabs. He concluded by reminding them that the Turks were encamped only a few miles north of their present position and asked if there were any questions.

A petty officer held his hand up and asked why, if they were there to protect the oil, they were going so far upriver from the wells and the pipeline.

The answer was that if they left Qurna in the hands of the Turks it would, apparently, be the perfect place from which to mount a strong attack on the oil installations. So the general in charge of the operation had decided they ought to capture and control it, which they had before *Clio* arrived.

As they went down the ladder to their messdeck Archie and Phil agreed that they had to get ashore to see this Garden of Eden. And so the next day, dressed in their uniforms, they and others landed in a ship's boat on a stone jetty for a walk around the small town.

Near the jetty dates grew on tall palm trees, apparently available for anyone to pick. Then they reached the first buildings, which were little more than hovels made of dried mud and reeds. From them the sullen faces of the women, often scarred with smallpox, stared out before turning back to deal with iron cooking implements. They remained in the back of the mud dwellings. At the entrances to the dwellings men drew smoke into their mouths from long pipes connected to glass bulbs. Through these air bubbled, flavoured by the tobacco on top of the vertical tube that rose from each of them. Phil noted that it was the women who appeared to be doing all the work while the men took it easy.

Archie ventured the opinion that the pipes were called hubble-bubbles, although he wasn't sure. The two young men walked with confidence through the earthen streets. The Royal Navy of the day tended to walk with confidence anywhere. People knew better than to challenge them.

Looking between the buildings they saw raw sewage lying on the ground behind them as well as leftovers from meals past. The occasional donkey investigated such areas to see if it could glean food from what remained.

In the centre of Qurna the mud and reed buildings were replaced by single-storey stone structures but the overall feeling of the two boys was one of disgust. The Garden of Eden had turned out to be just a filthy slum.

As they returned to the ship they agreed that Adam and Eve had probably been glad to get out of it.

* * *

On 18 May 1915 in the House of Lords, Earl Kitchener, generally putting a positive slant on British efforts, summarized the state of the war:

In Mesopotamia our Indian soldiers have shown their value and bravery by attacking and utterly routing the Turkish forces sent against them. Sir John Nixon is following up the result of his victory, and the whole country is gradually being cleared of all hostile forces.

Kitchener added that he needed another 300,000 men to form new armies.

Chapter 13

A Punitive Expedition

Clio was now on a war footing. Her main tasks were to provide gunfire support for the army, and to deal with any Turkish gunboats that appeared down either of the rivers. However, there existed a network of reed-lined waterways to the north and west of Qurna that joined the Tigris and Euphrates. Along these it was suspected that both enemy spies and snipers were travelling.

As a member of a punitive expedition to deal with this Phil was detailed off to be one of the crew of the *Clio's* elderly steam cutter, on which was mounted a machine gun. They proceeded up the Euphrates and into some lakes through which the river flowed. The immediate target was a village of Marsh Arabs that had been actively hostile to the British Army. They had sniped at troops and in one case attacked and killed an entire reconnaissance party that had been attempting to identify the position of Turks in the vicinity of Qurna.

The naval lieutenant in command of the cutter had directions to the village of the Arabs concerned. It was to this that they steamed, arriving to see a number of men who knew retribution was about to be exacted and were seeking cover from the vessel. Phil was manning the machine gun mounted on the bows of the boat but by the time they were within range the only living things in sight were a herd of water buffaloes grazing close to the shore.

'Open fire!' ordered the lieutenant.

'What at Sir?' asked Phil.

'On the cattle – it's their food. Kill them. Get on with it!'

Taking a gulp Phil took aim and curled his finger around the trigger to spray a stream of bullets at the midriff of the nearest of the animals, which was quietly chewing its cud and looking at the boat. As it sank, dying, into the shallow water, Phil altered aim to another, and then a third. The innocent beasts didn't know what was happening and quietly sank down as one after another was killed by the stream of bullets from the machine gun. Eventually, the entire herd lay still or twitching as they expired, their heads drifting down into the waters of the shore.

'Didn't enjoy that, Gunn, did you?'

'No Sir' replied Phil, white-faced at the thought of what he had just had to do.

'Got to do it. These Arabs have got to know that if they are hostile they are going to catch it. If they play ball they'll be all right. They've been under the Turks for about 400 years. They ought to be glad we're here to get rid of them.'

Phil said he saw the reason but it did not make the memory of his task any more pleasant.

The punitive matter dealt with, the steam cutter turned into the canal-like waterways that led off the lakes to search for potential enemy. Phil secured the machine gun and started to regain some of his composure. It was the first time he had killed anything and he felt sick at the experience. Next time it might not get to him quite so much, he thought.

Reeds and other water plants grew thick just below the surface and tall along the edges of the canals so that it was not easy to find their entrances in what appeared to be a waterborne maze. The propeller was constantly in danger of becoming clogged by weeds. When this happened it was Phil's job to take his clothes off, plunge over the stern into the pleasantly warm water and tear the weeds from the propeller. They would chug along while the water appeared clear, stopping the propeller before the next patch of weed in the hope that the boat's inertia would carry it across. If not, a boat hook was used in the shallow water to punt them clear. Had they not been in a sort of no-man's-land looking for potential enemies it would have been quite an enjoyable task.

Eventually the weeds became so thick that Phil was required to remain seated on the stern, clad only in his shorts, ready to leap over each time the propeller fouled. On one occasion they had turned back from a dead end, in a canal, which was not easy as the waterways were little wider than the length of the cutter. Suddenly the chattering of foreign voices was heard. Were these the spies or snipers for which they were hunting? Or were they Arabs seeking retribution for the recent attack on their village by men of the *Clio*? Over the tops of the reeds came the sight of high poles obviously being used for punting. The machine gun was loaded, by another seaman this time, and brought to the 'Ready'. The officer in command cocked his revolver. The remainder of the boat's crew took cover beneath the gunwhale,[1] and they waited in quiet anticipation. That is, except for Phil, who happened at the time to be shivering, naked, in the waters of the lake, clearing the propeller yet again. They were strangers in an alien environment, in an unwieldy craft, while the unknown were obviously very much at home in this watery jungle.

The voices became more distinct and the pole tops nearer. The other boat appeared to be manoeuvring along another canal, its occupants obviously unaware of the boat-of-war lying in wait.

A face bobbed into sight through and above the reeds. It disappeared, and then reappeared with a second mahogany-coloured countenance. To Phil's boat's crew their features seemed to be wreathed in hatred. What would come first? Spears … arrows … shots? But *Clio's* men did not dare to open fire in case these men were innocent watermen.

What did come into sight were two sets of beautiful white teeth, two large red tongues and the sound of hilarious cackling laughter as the boatmen went on wielding the poles on their inoffensive business among the reeds.

Phil wondered what these Arabs had thought when they saw the navy's cutter, manned by strange seamen with loaded weapons, entangled among the weeds so far up a canal in Mesopotamia.

They ended their search of the waterways and came out into the lakes again, lost, having twisted and turned through many directions. They had a compass and a general idea of which way to go, but night fell and so they anchored and slept.

The following morning, aided by the boat's compass, they headed east to where *Clio* should be and sure enough she hove into sight in due course. This was too late for the cutter's engine, however, which, having suffered so much stress from weeds in its propeller, gave up the ghost some 3 miles short of the ship. It was a 'powerboat' so had no oars or paddles. There was only one thing to do; for those last 3 miles they struggled back, propelling their craft as best they could. They paddled with wooden gratings from the bottom of the boat and the boat's baler, perspiration running down their half-naked bodies. Greetings from their fellow sailors on board were particularly ribald at the sight they presented. Not for the first time, Phil realized that you needed a sense of humour to survive in the navy.

Note

1. Piece of wood running around the top of the boat's side.

Chapter 14

Conditions up the Tigris

And so *Clio* remained in the vicinity of Qurna with the front line of the army and her fellow sloops. The Persian source of the oil for Britain's fleet had been protected so far and the war in Europe still seemed far away.

There were dangers. The Turks, guided by German officers, were floating mines down the Tigris with the aim of disabling the Royal Navy's ships. The sloops, moored in the river, benefitted from their sailors' considerable ability with ropes and spars and rigged 'mine catchers' across their bows (see illustration). These prevented contact with the ships' hulls, none of which was damaged although the floating mines seriously disabled a pontoon bridge above Qurna. Sailors from other ships told Phil that at the start of 1915 the weather had been pleasantly cool and the ground comparatively firm underfoot when they went ashore. But the roots of dry rushes, jungles of dried reeds and occasional patches of swamp intersected by sluggish streams suggested things could be very different at other times. Those other times were now upon them as the water coming down the Tigris from the melted snow off the mountains in the Caucasus to the north started to flood the desert into a vast inland sea. Out of this rose hillocks and small inhabited villages built high enough to permit their survival through the flood seasons. Turkish snipers occasionally came near to the ships and shot at them at night but this was more of a nuisance than a danger. It was now May and despite the cold water off the Caucasus the weather had become intensely hot, temperatures rising well above 100°F (38°C). There were many cases of heatstroke among both soldiers and sailors. On one day alone 117 went down with it. The heat was greater in the ships, where spaces tended to be confined, than on the land.

* * *

Meanwhile in the Mediterranean, preceded by naval bombardments, a British Empire and French force had landed in the Dardanelles threatening Constantinople itself. It was a bold attempt to create a diversion from the Western Front in Europe, to support the Russians and perhaps even knock Turkey out of the war altogether.

The new army commander in Mesopotamia, General Nixon, pondered on the reference in his instructions to submit a plan for an advance on the capital, Baghdad. Why not? The Turks, after all, were distracted by the recent attack at the Dardanelles.

This was not in accordance with the thinking of the new Secretary of State for India, in London, Mr Austen Chamberlain. As far as Mesopotamia was concerned, he ordered, sticking to the original objectives of safeguarding Basra and the oilfields should remain the policy. However, he would not object to an advance up the Tigris to Amara, a further 70 miles above Qurna, if capturing it would add to the security of the oil supplies. Those on the spot thought it would as Amara was between Turkish forces and the oil pipeline.

Chapter 15

Townshend's Regatta

The river Tigris had risen to an abnormally high level in early 1915 and the desert north of Qurna, to which the army and navy had advanced, was almost entirely under water. Out of this peered a number of sand hills on which the Turkish Army had set up gun positions. If the British were to advance upriver towards Amara they would have to eliminate them and they had to do it largely by water. This was deep enough in the river for the sloops, too shallow across the desert for these relatively large vessels, and almost impassable to soldiers on foot. And so there commenced the adventure that came to be known as Townshend's Regatta.

On 31 May 1915 HM sloops *Espiegle* and *Clio*, together with a motley collection of armed launches, tugs, lighters, barges and paddle steamers carrying troops, steamed slowly up the river past Qurna. While General Nixon was the overall army commander in Mesopotamia, Major General Charles Townshend had taken over direct command of most of the fighting troops. Townshend, embarked in HMS *Espiegle*, in consultation with General Nixon had made unusual preparations for attacks on the Turkish strongholds north of the town.

Phil was interested to see that secured to the ships' starboard (right) sides were a fleet of *bellums*, Arab canoes that rose to a point at either end. In some cases two were lashed together with a tall metal plate fitted across their bows to protect the occupants from enemy gunfire. Other *bellums* were to be seen moving with difficulty through the reeds over to the right.

As HMS *Clio* approached the first enemy position on a hill to their left, out from her starboard side and around the stern swarmed a mass of *bellums*, into each of which soldiers from the Oxfordshire and Buckinghamshire Light Infantry had embarked (see illustration). Amid a spray of foam they advanced towards the beaches while the sloops bombarded the enemy positions with their 4-inch guns. Under this barrage the Ox and Bucks, as the sailors knew them, paddled their *bellums* shorewards as fast as they could.

As they neared the shore gunfire from the vessels was checked so as not to hazard the British troops. Able Seaman Phil Gunn watched, fascinated, as the soldiers beached their boats and tore up the hill to the trenches and gun emplacements, slaughtering the Turkish defenders with rifle and bayonet. There appeared to be some Gurkhas among the attackers and Phil saw them cast aside their rifles as they reached the trenches, whip out their beloved kukri knives and set about the enemy. After only a few seconds a short line of Turks, the remnant of the defenders, walked out with their hands up in surrender to go into captivity (see illustration). Phil had never seen anything like it. The same operation was repeated by Indian regiments at other defended hillocks surrounded by water. The threat of gunfire holding up the British advance from Qurna was now eliminated altogether.

By midday the sun was beating down and the heat was so extreme that a halt was called to the operation. That afternoon General Townshend issued operation orders for the next day's attack. Starting at 5.00 am the sloops would bombard the next Turkish stronghold before the army landed to take it.

The flotilla set out the following morning as planned, ships' guns loaded ready to attack the next Turkish base in support of the troops that would be landed to take it. Before they got there the first Royal Flying Corps aircraft that anyone had seen in Mesopotamia flew over them and dropped a message for the general. Aerial reconnaissance had revealed, it explained, that the enemy had fled and was proceeding north up the river as fast as they could go. Indeed, in the distance the advancing British could see smoke rising above the water from the departing enemy shipping. Two armed steamers were dispatched in pursuit.

But another factor had come into the campaign. The Turks were putting mines in the river Tigris that threatened to blow up the Royal Navy's vessels as they advanced.

It just so happened, however, that in the recent battle the captain in the Turkish Mining Engineers who had laid the mines had been captured. It seemed sensible to invite this officer to stand in the bows of the leading vessel as it proceeded upstream and, to avoid being blown up himself, explain in advance where the Turkish mines were and how they worked. 'A seamanlike precaution' the Senior Naval Officer (SNO) described it. There was no damage from mines.

Chapter 16

They Destroy a Turkish Gunboat

From the upper deck of HMS *Clio* Phil found himself studying the barren desert terrain. It had been mostly covered by a few feet of water farther downriver but now there was dry sand, from which the odd piece of scrub grew. This was not enough to feed the army's camels, which had been brought from India, so most of them had now been sent back there.

Phil saw primitive-looking Arabs working with equally primitive implements or tending their cattle. They waved the same friendly greeting that they had probably proffered to the Turkish forces that had passed that way. It said, passively, 'We are friends to anybody who will leave us alone.'

Phil found himself sympathizing with these indigenous tribal people. They had been ruled, unwillingly, by the Ottomans for 400 years; were the British anything other than another invader that had its own rather than their interests at heart? He recalled the words of the sophisticated Arab in the Basra café, and the rumours he had heard that the Arabs would strip of their goods and kill any foreigner who left himself in a vulnerable situation.

There was little time to muse on such things, however, as the general had ordered the navy in its sloops to pursue the fleeing enemy shipping. The task was not easy as the swiftly flowing river snaked back and forth across a shallow plain. The tall masts of the three sloops *Clio*, *Espiegle* and *Odin*, up one of which Phil had spent many uncomfortable hours in a barrel as lookout, were good viewing points but also made them conspicuous to any enemy.

Intelligence had revealed that a Turkish gunboat was standing by to attack the British forces. Such intelligence cut both ways as the native Arabs sold it equally to the British and the Turks to their best financial advantage. There was now excitement as the gunboat was sighted.

The Turk was slow in spotting the incongruous sight of three British warships steaming through the desert. The ships increased speed, opened fire and the gunboat, realizing it was outgunned, turned tail. Phil, at his action station as a member of a gun's crew, watched the scene between moments of intense activity loading the 4-inch projectiles. They passed the spot known as Ezra's Tomb, marked by a domed shrine among palm trees. Here the prophet Ezra, on his way from Palestine having arranged for the repatriation of the Israelites, had died and was buried.

It was a strange situation as the river wound in leisurely bends across the flat desert so that the Turkish gunboat and British sloops went back and forth about a mile apart lobbing shells at each other across the desert. Navigation was intensely difficult for the three British ships in these narrow, fast-flowing and largely uncharted waters whereas the Tigris was home to the Turk. However, the Turkish shelling was inaccurate and the Royal Navy achieved a number of hits. Eventually *Odin* grounded on a sandbank in the shallow water but *Clio* and *Espiegle* were able to keep going until dusk. The uncertainties of this darkening river with its constantly shifting bed caused them to call a halt and anchor at about 9.00 pm to await the rising of the moon. In their retreat the Turks had left behind lighters and Arab vessels full of welcome stores as well as soldiers who were made prisoners, captured by the crew of the *Odin*.

With the moon rising at about 2.00 am, *Espiegle* and *Clio* weighed anchor and proceeded upriver in pursuit. They believed they had lost their chance of sinking the enemy. Or had they? Through the darkness they could just discern a stationery Turkish gunboat. Not only that, but smoke was pouring from the boat's hull, and through the smoke could be seen flames. Having first fired some shells at her that met with no reply, they steamed up close to the vessel, which they now saw their gunfire had wrecked (see illustration). Her crew had obviously run her aground, abandoned ship and vanished.

Clio had damaged a propeller and the captain was having difficulty in manoeuvring her. Concerned that she should not be left aground in the rapidly shallowing river, the SNO, who was the captain of HMS *Espiegle*, ordered *Clio* to return to Basra. With difficulty they turned in the river to commence the voyage downstream. This could only be done by driving her stern into the muddy bank and letting the current carry the bows downstream. It had been the farthest point to where ships of this size had ever ascended the Tigris.

Chapter 17

An Arab's Anaesthetist

During the chase of the gunboat the attention of those aboard *Clio* had been drawn to the urgent gestures of Arabs in a *mahaila*, a large river sailing boat that they had steamed past. Now proceeding downriver they came across the *mahaila* a second time. Her crew again waved and gesticulated at the sloop and it became evident that they urgently needed a doctor. The ship's steam cutter, of which Phil was a crewman, was lowered with the surgeon on board and went to investigate. Problems of language prevented any conversation with the crew of the *mahaila* but the surgeon went below and called for a member of the boat's crew to assist him. As bowman of the cutter Phil could most easily be spared so clambered down into the interior of the boat. It smelled repugnant to the young man.

An Arab lay groaning on the deck of the hold. It did not need the heated explanations of crew members to explain that he had received some of the shot of a shrapnel shell in his face, as well as a bullet in the eye. There was nothing for it but an immediate operation – not only for medical reasons but because *Clio* had to proceed downriver quickly lest she be caught aground by a reduction in the depth of the water.

'Have you ever administered chloroform?' the surgeon asked Phil.

'No Sir.'

'Then hold this and when I tell you, dab plenty of it on the mask and jam it over his nose.'

The surgeon handed Phil a phial of liquid and a pad of cotton wool. There was no clean water with which to wash either hands or equipment.

'Go on.'

Phil sprinkled the chloroform liberally on the pad and applied it firmly to the nose of the injured man, who immediately passed out.

So with Able Seaman Gunn acting as anaesthetist, the surgeon went to work in the dimly lit compartment, removed a bullet from the casualty's eye and bandaged him up.

It was a pity, thought Phil, that the surgeon was unable to tell the patient's companions what to do next. But they had no time to see him regain consciousness so the medical bag was packed and they returned to the cutter and hence to *Clio*. But Phil was only to remain in *Clio* temporarily.

Chapter 18

Travelling with the General

The general had given the order to advance on up the Tigris and the troops had embarked in flat-bottomed steamers driven by a large stern paddle wheel (see illustration). Of shallow draught, these vessels would be able to negotiate the waters as the depth decreased upriver. The water level had been abnormally high, but it was now falling and the senior naval officer was keen not to risk the larger vessels becoming stranded. It appeared that the Turks were retreating fast, so, well above Qurna, the general and the SNO transferred to HMS *Comet*, a shallow-draught armed paddle yacht. They would pursue the retreating enemy and reconnoitre. *Espiegle* and *Odin* would join *Clio* in the deeper waters at Basra.

The *Comet* was short of hands and, with a number of other seamen and before *Clio* had gone too far downstream, Phil was temporarily transferred to her. It was a matter of surprise and interest to him that he found Major General Townshend also embarked. *Comet* proceeded upriver, stopping at the small town of Qala Salih early in the afternoon to gauge conditions at the larger regional town of Amara. It was their aim to capture this next. White flags of surrender were flying in Qala Salih on their arrival and the senior Arab citizens confirmed this surrender. Clearly the news that the force meant business had registered locally and they were told that the British would be their friends as long as they co-operated with them.

Arab community leaders came aboard for a discussion with the general over the traditional thick, black coffee with which an Arab meeting is conducted. Phil, who happened to be doing some cleaning in the vicinity at the time, overheard General Townshend ask the Arabs if they would have supplies ready for 15,000 troops who would arrive shortly. The young sailor was surprised at the request because he didn't think there were as many as 15,000 British and Indian soldiers already in Mesopotamia.

After the Arabs had left there was a commotion ashore close to the ship with, unexpectedly, two Turkish soldiers who were rushing along the jetty and hailing them. They asked to come on board but *Comet* was now crammed with people. The captain told them they could run away. At this they shouted indignantly that they were prisoners of war and, apparently, entitled to be captured. Eventually it dawned on the crew of the *Comet* that these soldiers knew they would certainly be murdered by the Arabs if left so they were allowed to come on board temporarily.

The small flotilla anchored for the night a few miles north of Qala Salih, going on towards Amara at 6.00 am the following morning, but trying in vain to get information about the retreating Turks from villages on the way.

Chapter 19

Amara Gives in to Nine Men

Thirteen miles south of Amara the SNO sent HMS *Shaitan* – a small armed tug – ahead to find out what was going on there. Like *Comet*, she was also undermanned. Phil, probably because he was only a temporary hand in *Comet*, again found himself transferred to her to make up the full complement of eight sailors. He was taken over to *Shaitan* in a motorboat, as usual with bag and hammock.

There might be military resistance at Amara so the plan was for the rest of the flotilla to stop just beyond the range of any Turkish guns while *Shaitan* reconnoitred. The general would then wait for the troops to catch up. These had been advancing in their paddle steamers some way behind, securing to the bank at night when it was impracticable to navigate the fast-flowing river.

The general, sharing the *Comet* with the SNO, was somewhat alarmed at being out in front of his army in the direction of the enemy. A keen student of Napoleon, he could not recall that great soldier ever having been placed in such a situation. He was eventually persuaded that as the Royal Navy had destroyed the other side's gunboat, its only real warship, and *Shaitan* was well ahead to give early warning of any enemy, he had little to fear. In any case, explained the SNO, their vessels could return downriver faster than any enemy troops could advance.

* * *

HMS *Shaitan* was a little flat-bottomed tug designed for river work but taken over by the navy. She was armed with a larger gun in the bows and a smaller one aft, which Phil Gunn had been told by the naval lieutenant in command to man. The other seven sailors had their own individual tasks about the vessel.

Phil was not quite certain what was happening except that they were ahead of the force and reconnoitring to find out what was happening at the next town upriver. As ordered, he manned and loaded his gun, making sure spare ammunition was ready to hand. Phil looked out at the banks with some trepidation as *Shaitan* steamed against the fast-flowing current.

Three miles south of Amara, which was on the right-hand[1] side of the river, the first buildings came into view. They looked better than the decrepit structures at Qurna. No enemy appeared in sight until they entered the straight stretch of water opposite the town. There they saw a floating bridge of boats, across which planks had been secured, crossing from one side to the other. The last of some enemy troops were walking across it from the town on the right to embark on a barge that was secured to a steamer on the left bank.

As they watched, the bridge of boats was opened and they could see the steamer and barge casting off to head through the gap upriver, presumably as part of the Turkish retreat.

'Twelve-pounder – two rounds only – target the steamer's bridge – open fire!' ordered the lieutenant in command of *Shaitan*.

Phil's opposite number on the forward gun swivelled it round, took careful aim and pulled the firing trigger to loose two shots, which crashed through the superstructure of the enemy vessel and exploded.

The Turkish troops in the barge behind the steamer rapidly disembarked and, throwing down their weapons, ran off up the left-hand bank.

HMS *Shaitan*, with the White Ensign of the Royal Navy flying proudly, steamed on. As it passed the town an extraordinary scene unfolded before Phil, who had been ordered to join the lieutenant and his temporary shipmates on the bridge.

Amara was full of Turkish enemy troops, about 500 of whom were emerging onto the right riverbank only a matter of yards away from them. When they saw *Shaitan* firing they turned round and ran back into the town. Several hundred yards on were hundreds more troops along both banks. *Shaitan* was practically surrounded by the enemy. However, they did not fire at the ship, possibly because they had seen what she had done to the steamer, and she carried on a further half-mile upriver. Here they came across another party of about 100 soldiers with six officers and called upon them to surrender, which they did. Phil was ordered to grab a loaded rifle and take the Turkish officers, with the whole party's weapons and ammunition, on board the tug. *Shaitan's* commanding officer then ordered the Turkish troops on the shore to march back along the riverbank abreast the vessel towards Amara and on the way they captured another 150 who melted out of the trees, threw down their arms in surrender and marched back to the town, sitting on the bank to await further orders.

The lieutenant[2] in command of *Shaitan* and eight sailors had captured 250 Turks, eleven officers and their weapons. They learned afterwards that they had also caused 2,000 Turkish troops, who could have annihilated them merely by standing their ground and firing at the little tug at point-blank range, to flee the city of Amara.

Notes

1. 'Right' indicates the bank on the right as seen from the advancing vessels and 'left' to that on their left throughout this book. This is for ease of understanding but is contrary to normal description, which is that right and left refer to the banks as seen from the flow of a river towards the sea.

2. Lieutenant Mark Singleton RN of the *Shaitan* was awarded the Distinguished Service Order for his contribution to the unopposed capture of Amara. The *Official History of the War in Mesopotamia* says: 'Greater daring than that of the *Shaitan* can hardly be imagined.'

Chapter 20

Amara Formally Surrenders

Well behind the *Shaitan*, the *Comet*, with both general and senior naval officer embarked, had been cautiously following up, leading the remainder of the small flotilla towards Amara, which they now entered. They had heard the explosions as *Shaitan's* 12-pounder shelled the Turkish steamer. As the little tug had not retired downriver for help and as no enemy guns had opened fire they assumed that all was well but it was an uncertain situation. Crowds of local people were assembled on the waterfront, along which several river craft abandoned by the Turks were lying.

The flotilla, which consisted only of *Comet*, two small armed tugs of which the *Shaitan* was one, and two small launches, anchored with its guns covering each approach to the town. Into this more Turkish troops appeared to be pouring in some disarray from the east.

The situation now was that a mere fifty officers and men were trying to control thousands of Turks and Arabs. These had been led to assume that vast British Army was on the point of arrival and didn't know it was in fact many miles behind.

Phil pondered on how few of them there were compared with the enemy they were supposed to be guarding. But these Turks, he was later to learn, were thoroughly demoralized at having been continually defeated, both up and down the river and across towards the vital oil pipeline at Ahwaz, in Persia, from which area they had been driven. Furthermore, the Turkish soldiers knew that the Arabs would have no hesitation in turning against whatever side happened to be losing, stealing their weapons and murdering them.

The senior naval officer in *Comet*, keen to keep up the illusion, sent a body of sailors ashore and had the Union Jack hoisted over the customs house. He posted a few sentries over some of the Turkish official establishments, hoping that hostile eyes ashore would not realize that these were the bulk of his entire force.

Soon the SNO received a message that the Turkish Governor of Amara and the Senior Turkish Military Officer wished to come aboard to surrender. The *Comet's* one remaining boat, manned by the only sailors left on board, went ashore for them and soon a procession of Turkish officers came along the quay in full dress uniform.

Townshend received them formally at the gangway speaking fluent French, displaying authority but also respect and affability. To emphasize the strength of his position he gave firm orders to the Turkish Governor to collect supplies for 15,000 men whose arrival, he indicated, was imminent. The Turkish dignitaries surrendered a large and varied collection of swords and pistols, symbols of their rank as well as fighting implements. They were politely given coffee. The British prayed that the Turks would not realize they were only fifty-strong.

There was a near miss when a Turkish naval officer revealed that he spoke English and it became apparent that he would have overhead the British discussing the weakness of their position. The SNO had him taken down below. The only available sentry to guard him was a Royal Marine lying on a camp bed recovering from an attack of fever. The bed was placed near the top of the ladder and the marine told that should the Turk try to come up he was to tell him to stop, and if he persisted, to shoot him. This cheered him up and he quickly felt better.

From the meagre force a naval lieutenant was sent with sixteen mixed sailors and soldiers who could be spared from the flotilla to keep order in the town. They marched briskly to the army barracks and there found a further 400 Turkish soldiers and officers, all fully armed, drawn up in the square ready to surrender. Pretending that this was what he was expecting, the lieutenant ordered them to leave their arms and forthwith marched them down to the waterfront guarded by the bulk of his small force. Fifty further Turkish soldiers marched up to the Turkish naval barracks and surrendered to the three British soldiers who had been left behind to guard it.

A lookout in the *Comet* reported to the SNO that there were about 2,000 more Turks coming in from the north-east. That busy officer, hoping he was succeeding in carrying out one of the biggest bluffs in military and naval history, told the *Shaitan* to fire some shells to disperse them. *Shaitan* fired. The Turks did run away but about fifty refused to as, they explained, they preferred IEF justice to that of the Arabs. The commanding officer of *Shaitan* made them hand over their arms and remain seated on the shore as prisoners, covered by the tug's guns.

Chapter 21

The Army Arrives Just in Time

Phil Gunn in the *Shaitan* wondered where they were going to put all these Turks. He knew that the army was not due to reach Amara for some time although urgent signals had been sent back to expedite its arrival.

Reasoning that the Turkish prisoners would mostly be unable to swim the senior naval officer commandeered a tug with a very large lighter that the Turks had left behind. Eight hundred men and eighty officers were embarked in this. It was moored out in the stream well clear of the banks, but in a position commanded by British guns. Others were similarly restrained in smaller barges. In all cases the Turks had been disarmed, many of their rifles having been thrown into the Tigris as there simply was nowhere to stow them in the little vessels.

The naval craft were moored in position for the night along the river and overlooking the town. A proclamation was sent ashore that the inhabitants were to remain indoors after sunset and that anyone seen in the streets would be shot.

The navy settled down anxiously for the night but as the next day dawned the Arabs in the town started to realize the true state of affairs and rioting commenced. It was held in check by machine-gun fire from the vessels offshore. However, in the night they had seen the lights of a steamer approaching and, sure enough, at about 10.00 am, one of the paddle steamers arrived with 700 of the Norfolk Regiment aboard. The vessel went alongside, covered by the flotilla's guns; the Norfolks tore ashore and soon brought the town under control.

When the numbers were finally added up, Townshend's Regatta had captured about 140 officers and 2,000 men. It had destroyed a Turkish gunboat and a tug as well as capturing two steamers, two tugs, two motor boats and ten iron barges. Also in the bag were twelve field guns, five naval guns, 2,700 rifles, more than a million rounds of ammunition and a large quantity of other stores.

They had done this with about fifty British sailors and soldiers in intense heat, plagued by mosquitoes and flies, at the height of the Mesopotamian summer.

* * *

Following the capture of Amara Phil was told to leave the *Shaitan* and rejoin HMS *Clio*. He was ordered into a steamer going down to Basra. A boat took him over from *Shaitan* and in a day or so he was back with his familiar messmates aboard the sloop.

His friend Archie asked what he had been doing. Phil explained that he had been transferred from *Clio* to the old paddle steamer *Comet*, then again to the little tug *Shaitan*. He described the approach to Amara, the capitulation of the Turkish troops they had found there and the capture of the town, alive as it had been with the enemy, for a somewhat envious Archie's benefit.

Chapter 22

Phil Volunteers for 'Hazardous Duties'

Phil was approached by Petty Officer Jock Bryce a few days after he arrived back in HMS *Clio*. Bryce told him that 'they' were looking for volunteers for 'possibly hazardous duties'. Did Phil want a bit of fun? Phil asked him what would be involved.

It was something to do with towing boats with guns in, explained Bryce. Phil put his name down and, with other seamen, was duly selected. Four barges, in each of which was mounted a large gun, were to be lashed either side of two former Calcutta River Police steam launches (see illustration). The barges were called horse boats as they had no engines and had previously been towed by horses walking along the bank of the Suez Canal. The 4.7-inch guns, although naval, had been landed and, it was said, used at the Relief of Ladysmith in the Boer War in 1899. These guns were to provide vital artillery support to the army when the river became too shallow for the sloops to proceed further. The purpose of having them towed by steam launches was that these shallow-draught vessels could manoeuvre inshore to secure them against the bank, thereby providing a stable gun platform. It ought to hold some excitement, thought Phil.

Each launch had an existing Indian crew of four. Lieutenant Commander Cookson of HMS *Clio* was to be in overall command and would be accommodated in RN2, one of the two launches, assisted by Phil. RN1 was to be controlled by Leading Seaman Thompson, who bore three good conduct stripes indicating twelve years of adult service. Seamen gunners would provide the gun crews and live in the horse boats, while Cookson, Phil and Thompson would be accommodated in their launches.

Phil and Thompson went in the *Clio's* steam cutter to inspect the launches and meet their Indian crews. Already somewhat top-heavy, the craft were now protected from sniper fire off the riverbanks by steel protection plates around the cabins and engine room casings. The engine room was amidships, beneath a cabin from which the vessel was steered.

The cabin also contained lockers for small arms and ammunition as well as a bunk for the person in command. Cookson would be in his launch so Phil expected to have to doss down with the crew, which consisted of an Indian coxswain, stoker and two seamen. They would be accommodated in a forward cabin under the upper deck.

Phil nodded to the Indian coxswain. He was a fine-looking man of medium height, wearing a turban and with an aquiline face that included a magnificent moustache. A loose grey cotton jacket hung over khaki shorts above bare legs and rope-soled shoes.

'We have to work together under an officer,' explained Phil. 'What is your name?'

'I am Abdul, Sahib,' replied the coxswain, who evidently spoke good English.

'No need to call me Sahib,' corrected Phil. 'I'm not an officer … just an able seaman. And my name's Phil.'

'I will call you Able Seaman Phil, Sahib,' replied the coxswain. 'And these are my crew.' He indicated two similarly dressed seamen and a small, gnarled man in a brown boiler suit who turned out to be the launch's stoker.

'Where is your home?' asked Phil. He asked more out of politeness than really wanting to know from where they came. But he felt it might be important to work up a good relationship.

'We are a boat's crew from the River Chenab, close to Multan in the Punjab,' was the reply, which left Phil none the wiser. The detailed geography of India had not been part of his education. However, these few exchanges suggested to him that he could work with these men, who looked as if they were willing to please and co-operate.

Phil and Thompson turned their attention to the nearest horse boat. These had steel sides, flat bottoms and rounded bows, behind which a small wooden deck carried an anchor. In the centre was the gun, peering out of a gun shield, and in the stern, a covered accommodation section surrounded by vertically stowed shells, plus a few lockers for stowage of personal effects. That was it.

The four 4.7-inch guns were to be a large part of the main armament to provide covering fire for the army's advance up the river Tigris. Each launch would tow two horse boats; one lashed each side of it.

'At least they're breech and not muzzle loaders,' commented the more experienced Thompson.

At this point they were joined by Lieutenant Commander Cookson, who had come to see what his charges looked like.

They learned that, at times to be directed by General Townshend's staff, the crews of the launches were to slip the horse boats. They would then manoeuvre them and, with the aid of the seamen gunners on board, secure them to the riverbank. Under the control of Cookson, Phil and his opposite number, Thompson, would manoeuvre their launches to lay out anchors from the horse boats into the stream so that they provided a stable gun platform. An army observation officer would come aboard and direct the fire of the guns onto the Turkish enemy as they, hopefully, retreated back up the Tigris.

Cookson seemed a little thoughtful. He walked around both horse boats and launches, looking at the cabin in the latter, and then came back to where Phil was standing.

'Look, Gunn, I think I am going to stay in one of the paddle steamers, the *Comet*, as we go upriver,' he said. 'I'll control things from there and keep in constant touch with you and Thompson, although I suspect the army will take you over in due course. You handle boats well. Are you happy to take charge of RN2 on your own?'

Phil hesitated before answering. He was still only an able seaman and here he was effectively being given a command, albeit a small one, which would involve taking charge of an Indian crew as well. He took a deep breath.

'Well – yes Sir. I'll have a go.'

'Good lad. That's settled then. We'll await orders to sail.'

Phil saluted. Cookson returned his salute and walked away, leaving Phil pondering why Cookson was not going to stay in RN2. He supposed he had been brought up in the relative comfort of a naval officer's wardroom with a cabin of his own, whereas Phil was used to slinging a hammock from the deckhead and living out of a kitbag and locker. Perhaps it was just that, as an officer, Cookson was not used to roughing it like the sailors. The young man went to get his bag and hammock and returned to RN2.

Chapter 23

Savagely Attacked by Mosquitoes

Phil settled himself into RN2, finding it an exciting novelty to contemplate his new living environment. He laid out his hammock and mattress on top of the cabin lockers on which he would sleep. In *Clio* the hammock had been slung from hooks in the deckhead. Phil rigged up his mosquito net above and around the sleeping area, for this would be indispensable at the height of the Mesopotamian summer.

Night fell when he went to *Clio* for his evening meal, returning to the launch to turn in. The seamen to man the guns in the horse boats were still living in *Odin* and *Clio* well above the surface of the water, whereas Phil was only a few feet above it.

He was unable to get much sleep that first night, the mosquito net adding to the already oppressive heat and humidity of Mesopotamia in June. After an hour or so of lying uncomfortably awake Phil folded the mosquito net away and endeavoured to doze off. Zzz … bing! A mosquito of seemingly enormous size had found him. Having slaughtered it he lay down again and hoped for better luck. But no, he seemed an easy prey for others who swarmed over the still water around the launch. There was nothing left to do other than replace the mosquito net and suffer the stifling heat, feeling uncomfortable yet smugly secure.

But Phil did not know his Mesopotamian mosquito. Before long the Zzz almost at his face heralded the fact that they had stormed his defences and were actually inside the net. Bing! He was bitten again …

How thankful he was to see the dawn appear, hot as he knew it would be later in the day. Phil was in acute discomfort from the attentions of the large insects that had attacked him during the night. He thought of their attacks as 'bites' but it would not have helped his state of mind had he known that they were in fact piercing his skin in order to suck his blood. In the cool of the early morning he set his Indian boat's crew to work in making the launch shipshape for the upriver journey he knew would commence shortly. They were working what the navy knew as tropical routine, from 7.00 am to 1.00 pm. The forenoon's work completed, Phil, more than ready for a sleep after his disturbed night and with no mosquitoes to worry him, followed the customary tropical routine of settling down for a siesta on his improvised bunk dressed only in vest and pants.

However, in no time at all he felt a sting on his leg. Mosquitoes? Surely not in the daytime. To Phil it seemed to be an ordinary looking large fly, which he squashed without difficulty. Back to doze again. Ping! Another sting … another fly … another death. But what a sting they had. They were female horse flies. They cut through Phil's skin with small scissor-like jaws, pushed the wounds open and then inserted a sucking tube to draw off his blood. He was not to know all this and as far as he was concerned the 'stings' were very painful. Phil stood little chance against them.

Almost in despair at his plight, the cause of which did not seem to be afflicting the launch's Indian crew, he was forced to put on some outer clothing. While subjecting him to intense heat, this seemed to keep the flies at bay, except that the thick woollen stockings had a thousand loopholes. Through these the flies continued to sink their fangs into him. His siesta came to an abrupt, uncomfortable end. At around 4.00 pm, for a short time there appeared to be relief from the flies and the stinging stopped. But it was a false relief for very soon came the now familiar, hateful mosquito Zzz of the previous night.

When it came time to turn in Phil knew there was nothing for it but to cover himself from head to foot with his blanket if he was to beat the menace of the mosquitoes, and this he did. He must have dozed for only a short while, waking with a start and a fearful sense of suffocation. He uncovered his face while the remainder of his body perspired freely, standing by to 'repel boarders' from face and neck. Then it was back to being totally covered by the blanket until the suffocation woke him again. And so it went on, all through the night.

Becoming more and more exhausted Phil implemented the blanket covering scheme against the flies the following afternoon but the heat of the day was too intense to suffer under the blanket for more than a few minutes at a time. As a young able seaman he had been trained in a culture that did not complain but 'got on with it', so there was no question in his mind of going to a higher authority, asking for help and saying he could not stand it any more.

Mosquitoes by night, horse flies by day. Was he never, then, going to get any sleep? After a few days of this torture he wondered as he lay under the blanket, how will it end? How can I stand it? What is this feeling of despair? Am I really going mad?

Phil's appalling conditions lasted while the launch was alongside at Basra. He had realized by now that the climate and pests of Mesopotamia were going to be a great handicap to him and his fellow sailors. They would, however, be allies to the enemy, who were more or less born to them.

At last, one morning came the order to cast off and proceed. They got under way and went to the horse boats, one after the other, securing each alongside in turn. They moved away from the stagnant air of Basra. To Phil's immense relief the increasing speed of the launch as it gathered way breathed fresh air into its windows. They left the mosquitoes and horseflies behind.

The burden of the two unwieldy horse boats made the manoeuvring of the launch difficult for the Indian coxswain. Phil, who by now had much experience at boat handling, found himself having to stand ready to give guidance, or indeed take over the wheel so that they remained under control. They steamed on upriver, accompanied by other vessels. They passed Qurna and eventually reached Amara, with which Phil was familiar, having taken part in its daring capture, although he had not yet been ashore there.

Chapter 24

A School Friend

A lieutenant came over from the *Comet* in which the senior naval officer was embarked. He had a message for Phil that his launch and the horse boats were to come under the command of the army from now on. Phil and the sailors manning the guns in the horse boats would draw their provisions from the army quartermaster.

The lieutenant added that the current in the river was growing stronger as they headed upstream. So the horse boats would now be towed by the paddle steamers with their stronger engines on the longer stages upriver. Phil, in RN2, would steam in company, standing by to manoeuvre his horse boats when required.

Amara looked a good town, he thought. Turkish soldiers had either been captured or had fled and the resident Arabs, theoretically neutral, appeared to be going about their daily business. A long line of well-built houses stood behind an attractive river front on the right-hand side looking upstream. This was the first real contact with the shore that Phil had had for some time so it was a good opportunity to get ashore and stretch his legs. He encouraged his Indian crew to do the same. They also took in fresh provisions supplied by the army quartermaster. Phil had previously joined the sailors in the horse boats for his meals, cooked on their stoves especially fitted for the purpose. However, now that these were to be towed by the steamers, except when he would manoeuvre and secure them to the bank, he would have to cook his own meals. This would be on the coke-fired vertical stove fitted to the stern of the launch and on which the Indian crew also cooked their food. So he bought himself a copper frying pan without a handle. Amara frying pans didn't seem to have handles. He also bought a saucepan, which did.

It was good to be able to land and walk around the covered market where, already, locally manufactured jewellery, beaten copper utensils and textiles were on offer to the British and Indians passing through, despite the place having only recently been a war zone. Phil passed a fresh meat stall, somewhat concerned at the quantity of flies that were feasting off the meat on display. His unspoken question as to what meat was on offer was answered when he noticed the head of a dead camel hanging over the stall.

Native market places were always interesting; they enabled him to compare one country's way of living with another. Some men wore headdresses of wound cloth, a little like the turbans of the Sikh soldiers in the Indian Army and his launch's crew. Others wore pieces of black and white check material called a *keffia*, held down onto their heads with an *agal*, a circular double black woollen band. All wore loose-fitting robes that went down to the ground. In among them were a few who wore jacket and trousers, and a red fez on their head. Phil presumed these were Turkish merchants and therefore non-combatants. There seemed to be very few women in the market.

Here and there craftsmen bent over something they were making to sell, protected from the strong sun by awnings.

Outside the lines of the market small children played and smiled at the foreign strangers who were no threat to them. One or two raised their right hand in a salute in the manner of the soldiers and sailors they had seen. Though they went barefoot, Phil thought that most of the children looked clean and well dressed even though their clothing differed vastly from that he was used to.

At one corner of an alley Phil came across a group of four young British soldiers.

'Hullo, Jack,' was the friendly greeting of one, using the nickname with which British sailors were addressed the world over. 'Where are you from then?'

'Teddington.'

Another of the soldiers started, looked and pointed at Phil. Phil looked back and, to his astonishment, recognized a former school friend. It was Jim White, known – as were all 'Whites' in the British services – as 'Knocker', whose family lived at Kingston, close to Teddington.

'Who are you with then, Knocker?' asked Phil.

'The Dorset Regiment.'

'But you don't come from Dorset. You're from Kingston.'

Knocker explained that his family had moved to Dorchester, where his father had got a job gardening at a big house. Knocker's friends moved on, browsing along the stalls down the adjoining alley.

Phil asked him how he was getting on with the Dorsets. Knocker said they were a good bunch but he hated the heat and flies. Phil agreed that the flies were awful and the mosquitoes even worse. He asked Knocker if he had seen much of the Arabs out in the desert. They hung around over the horizon waiting to see what pickings they could get, said Knocker, who considered the Arabs a slimy lot. He and his colleagues preferred the Turks. At least you knew where you were with them.

Phil asked him whether he had seen any fighting and Knocker explained that they had been among the first British troops to land down on the Shatt al Arab. He had been involved in the infantry fighting and had bayoneted and killed a Turkish soldier there. Knocker qualified his achievement by conceding that he had not been a very big Turk. Nevertheless, Phil was impressed.

Phil explained to Knocker that he had been put in charge of a launch with an Indian crew towing boats with guns to support the army. Would he like to come and see it?

But Knocker had to get back to his regiment and there was not time. They agreed to try to keep in touch.

Chapter 25

His Muslim Crew Need Halal Meat

There were some huts across the river at Amara and as Phil had seen Arab women who inhabited such dwellings trying to sell fresh eggs he asked his coxswain if he thought they might have any to sell.

Abdul thought they would and it was agreed that Mohammed, one of the crew members, should accompany Phil on an egg-shopping expedition. Abdul gave a brief order to Mohammed, who got himself ready to go with Phil up to the bridge of boats and across to the other side.

They walked down the riverbank, passing the huts until they came to one with hen coops behind it. Two Arab girls, dressed in loose black robes and headscarves woven from goats' hair that left their faces and lower legs exposed, smiled at them discreetly. One politely gestured that they had chickens and eggs to sell. Phil had almost forgotten what women were like, having seen virtually none since he had left China, and warmed to their welcoming look.

Phil asked Mohammed to enquire how much they wanted for a chicken. The Indian muttered something to the girls in Hindi and one answered him in Arabic, but somehow they seemed to understand each other. Mohammed turned to Phil and explained that the price was four annas for a chicken and one anna for four eggs.

This was Indian money, which Phil had used a little in Basra, but whereas he was used to Indian rupees, annas were unfamiliar. He told this to Mohammed and asked if he knew how much that would be in English money.

With an unexpected knowledge of currency the Indian explained that there were sixteen annas to the rupee and fifteen rupees to the pound. So a chicken would cost six pennies and eggs one and a half pennies each. This sounded perfectly satisfactory to Phil, who told him to ask for a chicken and eight eggs.

Although friendly, the Arab girls' smiles were shy in the presence of the invaders. Phil sensed that they would have given them both eggs and chickens for nothing if pressed. These were peaceable people, to his eyes, just grubbing along in the only type of existence they knew, overrun by a foreign power again, whose army would require the foodstuffs that were probably only just sufficient for their own needs. They gave the girls the money and walked back to the launch. A chicken with flapping wings dangled from the Indian's hands by its legs and the eggs were in a small reed basket.

Phil approached the coxswain on their return and asked if one of the crew could kill and gut the chicken for him. Home for him was the suburbs of London and he was not a country boy used to such activities while Abdul and his men had their own separate food and cooking arrangements.

Abdul expressed his willingness to arrange this but then went on to say that he and his crew had a problem about which he must speak to Phil. Phil listened carefully as the coxswain explained that the army quartermaster issued them with meat that had been killed by – and Abdul asked forgiveness for putting it like this – an infidel. But he and his fellows were Muslims and their religion did not permit them to eat meat killed in this way. They had done so far because the Quran said it was not sinful if Muslims were forced to eat it if there was nothing else, but his boat's crew were devout men and were very unhappy about it.

This was a new one for Phil, who, nevertheless, said he would see what he could do. And so the next morning he went along to the quartermaster's store and raised the matter with the burly corporal behind the counter.

The soldier raised his eyes to the heavens in a gesture that implied, 'Oh God, not another one'. But in reality it was not a problem as the QM was already supplying the Indian Muslim regiments in the campaign with live sheep and goats for slaughter and consumption. He agreed to let Phil have one sheep a fortnight.

And so it was arranged that a crewman from RN2 launch would go to the stores every other week and draw a sheep to lead back on board the boat. When the meat was required the sheep would be duly bled, slaughtered in halal fashion, cut up, some eaten fresh and some preserved in salt so that it would not go bad in the heat. Phil did not go into whether his crew were allowed to eat beef but was relieved that the issue never arose. Stowing a live cow in their small craft would have presented serious problems.

Phil himself became a beneficiary of the sheep arrangement as he was invariably presented with one of the legs, which he boiled on top of his vertical stove in the stern. Indeed, practically every time he needed to cook something all he knew what to do was to boil it in his newly acquired saucepan.

Boiling was in river water, which they drew and poured into an earthen *chatti*, where it was allowed to settle and cool, after which it looked all right. Phil always added one of the purifying tablets with which they had been issued but his Indian crew never bothered with them and did not seem to suffer. For peace of mind it was necessary to ignore the bodies of the dead soldiers from both sides that they occasionally saw floating down the Tigris.

When the arrangement had been made for the army to take over the horse boats and the launches that towed them, a deputation of seamen from the boats had gone to Lieutenant Commander Cookson of HMS *Clio*, who had administered them to date. The sailors pleaded that their rum should still come from the navy, whose rum quality was considered to be superior to that of the army, and this was agreed.

As Phil was the only teetotaller among them, the sailors who manned the guns in the horse boats had elected him to draw and keep their rum ration, issuing it daily as King's Regulations decreed. Each got one-eighth of a pint, a considerable slug of rum, mixed with two parts of water. This was not solely to weaken its impact but it also prevented sailors saving up their 'tots', as they were called, and embarking on a drunken orgy at the end of the week. These had been known to be fatal.

A certain amount of drunkenness did take place when somebody had a birthday. It was then the tradition that everyone else in the birthday boy's boat would allow him a sip of their tot. They would watch as he took his sip and the cry would go up 'Sippers, not gulpers!', if it was felt their generosity was being abused.

Phil was happy to be keeper of the rum, but he also decided to draw and keep his own ration neat in a separate bottle instead of taking the few extra pence that abstention would bring. When he had accumulated about half a pint he would take it to the corporal at the quartermaster's counter and trade it for something extra, such as half a side of bacon. It was a useful barter. He sometimes wondered who had 'lost' the bacon but saw no soldiers who looked as if they were going hungry, though many suffered from various other ailments in this difficult Mesopotamian climate.

Chapter 26

Nixon Presses the Case for Baghdad

The Indian Expeditionary Force had come to Mesopotamia to protect the navy's oil supplies near Basra. However, murmurings were increasing that the eventual aim might be to capture Baghdad, the capital of Mesopotamia and some 570 miles up the river Tigris from the sea. So despite the Admiralty's insistence that protecting the oil was paramount, this priority was receding in overall Army Commander General Nixon's mind. The prospect of the far grander aim was taking over.

Nixon was also influenced by the apparent invincibility of British forces in Mesopotamia, who had won everything to date. And he was a general in, after all, the army of the largest empire the world had ever seen.

One hundred and fifty miles up the Tigris above Amara was the larger town of Kut al Amara. It lay on the eastern bank and opposite it a smaller river called the Shatt al Hai diverted from the main stream. The Hai meandered across the desert of Lower Mesopotamia in a southerly direction, eventually joining up with the large river Euphrates that ran down to join the Tigris north of Basra.

General Nixon considered the Hai a possible danger. It could enable the Turks to travel by water, usually easier in Lower Mesopotamia, across to the Euphrates, down which they could launch an attack on Basra. However, if Nixon's forces took Kut al Amara, or as it was usually abbreviated, 'Kut', he could prevent use of the Hai in this way. His reasoning overlooked the fact that the Hai was generally much too shallow to take troop-carrying vessels and so was not really a threat.

The taking of Kut would also bring the IEF closer to a position from which it could launch an attack to capture Baghdad, Nixon's grand aim.

The newly appointed Secretary of State for India, in London, Mr Austen Chamberlain, was anxious about Nixon's intentions and wrote to the Viceroy of India, Lord Hardinge: 'I hope that Nixon realizes how short you are of troops and the extreme difficulty there would be in reinforcing him.' Britain was, after all, fighting a major world war in Europe.

Nixon put his proposal to capture Kut up to Lord Hardinge using his argument that it would prevent the Turks from using the river Hai. If we captured Kut, Nixon said, this would avoid us having to divide our forces and defend against Turks possibly coming down both the Tigris and the Euphrates. A few days later he produced a further reason for occupying Kut. It would improve our position greatly in regard to the difficult tribes along the Tigris, whose habits were both predatory and treacherous. However, as others realized, to take Kut would extend our lines of communication from the sea, already 200 miles distant, by a further 150 miles.

Mr Chamberlain in London reiterated the Admiralty's concern that no interruption of their oil supplies should take place and urged restraint. However, Lord Hardinge, now persuaded, replied that, all things considered, the occupation of Kut was a strategic necessity and would contribute to the safety of the oil supply. Nixon was, accordingly, given the go-ahead to march on Kut but he made it clear that if problems arose around the oil fields he could not take Kut and protect them as well. The aims of the campaign were surreptitiously changing.

General Nixon also gave it as his opinion that Middle Eastern unrest would best be countered by advancing on Baghdad. For him to hold that city he would need an extra army division, by which he probably meant about 8,000 troops, and suggested withdrawing that number of Indian troops from Europe. Lord Kitchener, Secretary of State for War, in London, said he couldn't have them.

Chapter 27

What's Happening in Mesopotamia?

There was concern among some in Britain that very little news was emerging about the campaign in Mesopotamia. On 5 July 1915, General Sir Ivor Herbert MP described words that were not understood by the British public as 'having about as much meaning to the man in the street as the word Mesopotamia'.

In the House of Commons on 21 July, a Mr T.M. Healy MP asked the Under-Secretary of State for War why no dispatch or official report of the operations in the Persian Gulf had been published. Was it intended to publish any report dealing with the operations commenced in November 1914? If not, were the services of the officers and men of the forces so engaged to go without recognition?

Mr Tennant, the under-secretary concerned, replied that dispatches regarding the operations in Mesopotamia had been published in the *Gazette of India* on 26 February. Further dispatches had been received and were being considered by the Government of India with a view to their publication. He was discussing with the Admiralty and War Office the desirability of reproducing these dispatches or their substance in the *London Gazette*. In any case, he hoped to take steps to ensure due recognition of the services of the officers and men whose work had been commended.

But nothing happened.

Clearly, letters were filtering home about the conditions and illnesses from which some of the troops in Mesopotamia were suffering. Constituents wrote to their MPs.

In the House of Commons on 26 July the Secretary of State for India was asked whether he had any recent information concerning the health of our fighting men in Mesopotamia: whether many of them were suffering from fever or the result of exposure to the excessive heat, and whether there were adequate hospital accommodation and sufficient hospital comforts for sick men.

Mr Chamberlain replied:

It may be said that the health of the troops in Mesopotamia is good. There were during June twenty-seven cases and nine deaths from enteric [typhoid] but there has been no special prevalence of enteric at any time.

The heat has been, and is, intense but every effort has been made to minimize its effects. The troops have been supplied with spine protectors and goggles, mosquito nets and veils, and fans have been fitted in buildings where possible. There is ample hospital accommodation and a good supply of comforts for the sick.[1]

* * *

Things were not going well for Britain in the Dardanelles. In late August 1915, Austen Chamberlain had written to the viceroy, Lord Hardinge, that the situation there was, indeed, critical. Hardinge replied in mid-September, asking him to bear in mind that the capture of Baghdad would have as great an effect in the Middle East as success in the Dardanelles. However, he hesitated even to consider such a policy unless a reserve of troops was available.

As has been seen, Lord Hardinge had been influenced by General Nixon, who claimed there would be military, political and commercial advantages in an early occupation of Baghdad. He considered the troops at his disposal would probably be sufficient, although to hold Baghdad he would require reinforcements. To achieve his aim Nixon had urgently requested more river transport, including hospital vessels, to get troops and equipment up from Basra. The authorities in India and Britain had been unable to supply this but despite its absence Nixon persisted in his ambitions to advance.

General Townshend, the general in the field under Nixon, the army commander, saw things differently. He felt that having taken Kut, the force should hold on to what it had got in Mesopotamia and not advance further.

Note

1. Mr Chamberlain could only provide information sent to him by authorities on the spot. Later in the year, a statement by Mr Chamberlain that ice and other comforts were being provided in a hospital for the troops in Mesopotamia was described to him in a letter from an officer there as 'all eyewash'. Chamberlain accordingly urged the viceroy not to be content with easy assurances.

Chapter 28

Phil to Lead the Entire Expedition

Lieutenant Commander Cookson of the *Clio* came across to see Phil at Amara. In the temporary absence of the senior naval officer of the force, the captain of HMS *Espiegle*, which had returned to the deeper water downriver, he had taken over as SNO.

'Gunn, I've got a new job for you. It's too shallow for the sloops upriver and the water level will fall from now on so they've had to go back down towards Basra. You are already under the army administratively so that's all sorted, but there's another thing. The troops will continue up the Tigris in these shallow-draught paddle steamers. Your horse boats will be towed by one of these, the *Shusan*. I want you to take launch RN2 50 yards ahead of the leading ship. Is that clear so far?'

'Yes Sir,' replied Phil hesitantly.

'You are to get your boat's crew to make soundings as we go along. You must keep RN2 in the deepest channel all the time. The larger vessels will follow you and so will always be in the deep water, and won't run aground. We have to do this as the charts are not good and the riverbed changes all the time anyhow. Now I know you're only an AB but we think you can do this. Do you?'

'Yes Sir,' said Phil, a little uncertainly.

'Good lad. I'll be in one of the armed paddle steamers, so not far away.'

'So you mean … that effectively I'll be leading the Mesopotamia expedition?'

'That's right. Off you go now. We sail in about twenty minutes. You've got sounding poles haven't you?'

'Yes Sir.'

Phil, still only twenty, was relieved to learn that Cookson, in whom he had great faith, would be around for what sounded like a demanding new role. He called his coxswain over to explain it.

Abdul's chest swelled with pride as he thought that, as they would now be leading it, they were to be in charge of the entire expedition. Phil felt it necessary to put him right by pointing out that their role was merely to see where the water was deepest so that the larger vessels did not run aground.

Phil bade a cheerful but temporary farewell to the gun's crews in the horse boats. He ordered his Indian coxswain to steer RN2 past the rest of the naval flotilla and paddle steamers, now carrying 500 troops each, horses and all the supplies required by the army. Phil got his two crewmen to break out the 12-foot long poles used for sounding the depth and stationed one on either bow. He briefed them on their job of carrying out regular soundings of the depth as they proceeded upstream. Phil would note the depths, which were marked in feet on the poles.

They took up their position ahead of the flotilla and turned upstream.

'Keep her about 50 yards ahead of the bow of the first steamer,' Phil ordered the coxswain. 'I'll direct you for courses to steer.'

And so he found himself leading the British Indian Expeditionary Force up the river Tigris. The first of some biplane aircraft had arrived in the area and these carried out reconnaissance, reporting to the general on the movements of the enemy, who appeared to be fleeing upriver towards Kut al Amara, 150 miles ahead.

The further upriver they steamed, the swifter became the current, the shallower was the water and more frequently the sandbanks on the riverbed had moved. Sometimes the river widened when the water became even shallower. The vessels then had to zigzag across it according to where the deep water lay as well as conforming to the natural winding of the Tigris. They manoeuvred as depth was dictated by Phil's crew's sounding poles.

At the end of the first day the expedition anchored and Phil was exhausted. He'd had to concentrate for every minute, the weight of responsibility for stopping the expedition from running aground bearing heavily on his young shoulders. It was not feasible in these river conditions for the expedition to advance at night. He and his crew ate some cold mutton and turned in.

Chapter 29

They Land the Army

A siren at first light woke them up. It was General Townshend telling the expedition that it was time to proceed. The strange assortment of armed paddle steamers, launches, tugs and converted steam yachts weighed anchor and proceeded for another day in pursuit of their enemy. Phil found himself less tired today. Somehow his system had got used to the routine of sounding the riverbed. Occasionally he would take over from one of his Indian crewmen and carry out the work himself to give them a respite and him a change.

As he got used to the task his mind went to the situation in which the expedition found itself. They were in the middle of a desert, halfway between the Persian Gulf and the Turkish headquarters of Baghdad. The vessels were in the middle of a river with nowhere to go except up and down that river. It was a strange situation in which someone from the seagoing Royal Navy should find himself.

Another thought struck him. The space in the paddle steamers had been used principally for fighting men, eliminating non-combatants as much as possible. This had become evident to Phil at Amara when he had developed a septic finger and experienced difficulty in finding a medical officer to give him the treatment he needed. Eventually he did find one, but the lack of medical facilities gave him cause for thought. What would happen if many were wounded in any future action?

He had asked about this and noted the concerned frown that flitted across the medical officer's face. Tents would be erected to deal with any sick or wounded, it was explained.

On the afternoon of the third day a British seaplane landed near the leading paddle steamer. A boat was lowered and put out from the steamer to get a message from the pilot of the plane, which took off almost immediately, passing RN2 and leaving a flurry of foam in its wake.

Half an hour later, the same boat came up alongside RN2 and its coxswain shouted across.

'We're going in to the bank and putting the army ashore about an hour before sunset tonight. Arab village called Ali Gharbi. Keep a lookout for the order.'

Later, and with the sun low in the western sky, two short blasts were heard from the siren in the leading steamer just astern of RN2. Phil looked around and saw the vessel's bows swinging to the left. 'He's turning to port and going to run into the shore,' he said to the coxswain. 'Chosen this stretch because it's a bit deeper than what we've been through.'

Phil knew what he had to do and ordered his coxswain to steer across to the horse boat, which was being towed behind the steamer. A seaman aboard the steamer cast off the tow and Phil and his crew secured the boat alongside the launch, its gun meaningfully pointing ahead. The procedure was repeated when the second was released from its paddle steamer, more ingenuity being required in manoeuvring the launch, which was already hampered with the first powerless hull. Greetings were exchanged with the seamen manning the boats and they talked about the probability that the bombardment role of the horse boat crews was about to be tested.

The leading paddle steamer, followed by the two others, ran in alongside the shore, where they were secured. It was just above a small Arab village, from which smoke could be seen rising into the evening sky. Doors to the interior were lowered onto the shore to create a slope down which troops poured, followed by horses and those carrying equipment.

The steamers were then sent off downriver to pick up more of the army. The naval flotilla, which now consisted of the *Comet*, two launches – each with its two horse boats – and two small armed tugs, anchored for the night.

Phil watched the soldiers erecting their tents ashore, lighting fires on which to cook and camping down for the night. Cavalry patrols had been sent out to watch for the approach of any enemy. Again Phil pondered on the fact that, in view of possible impending enemy action, there appeared to be no medical facilities. He and his Indian crew cooked their supper of boiled mutton separately on the vertical stove and the horse boat crews cooked in their vessels.

He sat down on the stern of the launch as he frequently did after the day's work was done, thoughts drifting to life at home. With all the excitement of war, the voyage to the Persian Gulf and being given control of the launch, life in Teddington seemed a world away. Ignoring the time difference, around now his father would be settling down to read the paper in the front room. It would probably be the *Richmond & Twickenham Times*. Mother, having cleared the tea things away and washed up, would be sitting opposite, probably mending some clothing. His elder sister Ida, now twenty four, would not be there as she was in service to a well-to-do doctor's family in nearby Hampton Wick. Younger brother Sidney, ten, would have been sent to bed. The eldest, half-sister Molly, was the offspring of his mother's earlier marriage to an army sergeant who turned out to be a drunkard and they had parted. Molly had emigrated to the United States, not having got on well with her stepfather. Phil liked Molly and had been sad to see her go.

What he did not know was that every now and again his parents had seen telegram boys come up to the front door of someone living in their vicinity. A small envelope would be delivered, the door would close, and a few minutes later the front curtains would be drawn. Another son had been killed, somewhere, fighting for his country.

Rolling out his hammock on the flat locker in the stern Phil turned in wondering what the morning would bring. He slept well under his mosquito net despite the heat.

Chapter 30

A Briefing for the Fight

The sound of bugles ashore woke up the naval flotilla at about 5.30 am. September was intensely hot by day, with temperatures of about 131°F (55°C) in the shade. So they worked a tropical routine, starting before dawn and doing nothing in the middle of the day. They put away their bedding and grabbed some breakfast. Phil suspected that something was up and, sure enough, after half an hour the SNO came around in a boat and boarded the launch.

'Jump aboard and gather round!' Cookson called to the seamen gunners in the two horse boats. They assembled aboard the launch.

'Now this is the start of the real action,' he explained. 'The Turks are entrenched about 60 miles up the river. The army's going to march up alongside the Tigris and deal with them. We want to capture Kut al Amara, which is just beyond that.'

He turned to the seamen gunners.

'Your job will be to provide gunfire support for the army, who haven't got much in the way of guns up here. Gunn in RN2 has to go ahead and make soundings so that the paddle steamers don't run aground. Then when the army needs gunfire support he will be told to collect you from being towed astern of the steamers. You will secure alongside the bank while the launch lays out anchors into the stream to stabilize the horse boats and give you a good gun platform.'

'How will we know what to fire at Sir?' asked the leading seaman gunner from one of the boats.

'I was coming to that,' went on Cookson. 'An army forward observing officer will come aboard one of the launches towing you to direct the shoot.'

He turned to Phil. 'You've got a long ladder, haven't you?' Phil confirmed that he had.

'Well, you'll need to lash it vertically in position for the observing officer to shin up so as to see the fall of shot and direct the guns. Rig up a small platform at the top for him to stand on.'

Cookson jumped back into his boat to go off to give similar instructions to Phil's opposite number, Leading Seaman Thompson, in RN1.

Phil told his coxswain to get underway. They returned the two horse boats to the sterns of the paddle steamers, which would tow them upriver, then steamed to their post ahead of the expedition ready to sound the depths again.

At 6.30 am they saw the soldiers assembling on the shore and marching off in their companies of about 100 at a time. To keep down casualties from heatstroke they would march only until about 8.30 am, rest in the heat of the day and then march again in the evening before stopping for the night.

Phil could see how tough the going was for the soldiers. The ground was rough and the heat, even early in the day, trying. He also noted that a large tent was remaining behind at Ali Gharbi for the soldiers who had already succumbed to the intense heat.

* * *

Phil looked at those opposite. They were a company of the Dorset Regiment and there, to his delight, was his old schoolmate Knocker White.

Phil called across a greeting. Under normal circumstances he would not have addressed a fellow serviceman marching along in a formal squad, but these were not normal circumstances and discipline was somewhat relaxed in the trying conditions.

A perspiring Knocker returned his shout with a complaint about the heat and mosquitoes and pointed out that it was 'all right for Phil out there with his life on the ocean wave'.

'We've got our fair share of mosquitoes and flies as well and it's hardly the ocean wave,' replied Phil laughing, but he could see that his friend's shirt was already wet with perspiration. He would not have minded seeing some salt water and feeling a breeze off it but had worked out the previous day that they were about 300 miles from the nearest sea.

Knocker tripped over a tree stump and was told by his sergeant to concentrate. He gave a wave and they stopped talking.

Chapter 31

The Forgotten War

L oved ones in Britain sent out newspapers to the soldiers and sailors in the Indian Expeditionary Force to keep them in touch with home. They read of the war in France and Belgium. Fighting had been tough and conditions in the trenches hard, but as well as the photographs of men at the front were others of the beautiful nurses who tended them in peaceful hospitals to which the wounded were conveyed. The September weather in France appeared to be idyllic.

Up the river Tigris there had been and would be again tough fighting. But there were neither nurses, beautiful or otherwise, nor hospitals. At this time of year the temperature could be a humid 140°F (60°C) in the sun. There were flies by day and mosquitoes bit them savagely by night. The papers told nothing of such matters.

In London, *The Times* on 10 September 1915 commented on the lack of information coming out of government departments:

It is difficult to understand why the gallant work of the considerable British forces now engaged in Mesopotamia should be so sedulously veiled. The operations at the head of the Persian Gulf have now become widespread, perhaps too much so. These scattered bodies of men have faced much fighting, the fiercest heat and a very great deal of sickness. The country ought to be told more about the successes they have won, the hardships they have endured, and the very serious difficulties which still lie before them.

A letter in the same paper quoted a soldier up the Tigris who said that he saw fellows of his own service in France: 'having their deeds rewarded within two or three days. It would greatly hearten our troops here to feel that they were not completely forgotten in the tumult of events close at hand.'

A practical problem was shortage of vegetables, which was starting to cause both scurvy and beriberi among the British and Indian fighting men. Among other symptoms these could result in bleeding of the mouth, gums and general debility.

The man ultimately responsible for supplies was the army's quartermaster general in India, who was approached by a political officer on sick leave from Mesopotamia.

'I hear you are back from Mesopotamia,' began the QMG. 'I suppose you are full of grouses like everyone else there.' On hearing of the lack of vegetables and its consequences his reaction was, 'That's what they all say,' adding fiercely, 'What I always say is – if you want vegetables – *grow 'em!*'

This attitude highlighted a problem that was to affect much of the Mesopotamia campaign in its early stages. It was controlled from British India by politicians and officers who had often served in that country for years and been slowed down by the effect of its enervating climate. A whisky and soda on the verandah at Simla as the sun went down was an infinitely more attractive proposition than a journey up the Tigris to find out what was really going on. The navy were slightly better off than the army in this respect as they were controlled by the Admiralty in London, and could take their ships off to Bombay or Colombo to refit and replenish. This allowed the sailors, for most of the time cooped up in airless ships, to revitalize.

Chapter 32

The Mirage

For three more days the troops marched and the Royal Navy steamed upriver, resting in the heat of the day, proceeding in the early morning and evening.

Out to the left, the desert stretched to the horizon. In the far distance to the right, Phil could just make out the Persian mountains. Now that the spring floods from the waters coming down from the melting snows off them had subsided the land was largely dry but there remained permanent areas of marshland. Sometimes he could see the horizon but frequently, when the banks of the Tigris were high, they were visually cut off from the surrounding country.

On one occasion when the land lay flat from the river in all directions Phil found himself looking ahead of the army's marching column. To his concern he was alarmed to see an army of enemy infantry dressed in grey coming directly towards the British troops. He turned to the bridge of the leading paddle steamer astern of the launch, shouted a warning and pointed.

Binoculars were raised. After a few moments they were lowered and the voice of an army officer called out to him: 'It's all right. It's a flock of sheep.' It was Phil's first experience of the desert mirage, the bending of light rays that elongate and distort a distant object. The mirage could cause a group of donkeys to look like palm trees, infantry to resemble cavalry or a mud hut a fort.

On another occasion Phil saw a small group of British cavalry coming along the riverbank towards them. Strangely they appeared to be wearing armour as they had a metallic sheen all over them. He then realized that they were in fact covered from head to foot in shiny black flies and it was the reflection of the sun off these that he was seeing.

However, leading the expedition with the launch's sounding poles and ensuring the larger vessels were constantly guided into the deepest water,

Phil had little time to dwell on the view. The river was getting shallower. He needed to concentrate for every moment they were under way and now found himself in an almost permanent state of exhaustion. He seemed to have mastered the art of keeping mosquitoes at bay and slept soundly through the night, being woken for the expedition's early starts. The paddle steamers that had gone downriver to collect more troops now arrived with their contingents and disgorged them to join the gradually enlarging force.

Eventually Major General Townshend called a halt at a place called Sannaiyat. There was a small oasis of palm trees and the river was sufficiently deep close to the shore for the larger vessels to reach it. Phil was relieved that at last he and his crew were probably going to be able to catch up on some sleep, which they did that night. The hard-pressed soldiers did the same ashore, their tents having been carried along either in the paddle steamers or on the backs of mules. For several days the expedition rested.

But not all of them.

Chapter 33

The Attack on Kut al Amara

erial and naval reconnaissance had revealed that 8 miles ahead of them, protecting the town of Kut al Amara, the Turks had dug themselves into a strong defensive position. It was at a place called Es Sinn, their trenches going out at right angles on either side of the river. On the left they were set in a high and level bank that would force the expedition to attack across an open plain, with no cover and in full view of the enemy. On the right the Turkish trenches appeared to stretch from the river out to marshes that would also make a British advance difficult. However, a cavalry reconnaissance sent out by Major General Townshend revealed that there was a gap between two of these marshes. If he could get his troops through this gap they could come upon the Turks from the side and rear rather than trying to attack their trenches from the front.

It was important not to reveal this plan to the Turks and so the general placed a significant proportion of his soldiers on the left-hand side. His plan was to suggest an attack here to force the Turks to keep defending it, but at the last moment to move these troops across the river at night to attack between the marshes on the right.

The general ordered a number of *danaks* – large sailing boats used on the rivers of Mesopotamia – to be bought from Arabs downstream and brought quietly up to just below the British forces. Late one afternoon, and just out of sight of the Turkish front line, a floating bridge consisting of these *danaks* with boards stretched across them was discreetly assembled across the river. Phil, now under the control of the army, had been ordered to take RN2 and the horse boats up above the floating bridge alongside the front line troops and await orders.

That night most of the British soldiers on the left-hand side of the river, having given signs of great activity and carried out some brief attacks on the Turks, quietly crossed to the right. Their colleagues already on that side headed out away from the river to find the gap between the marshes

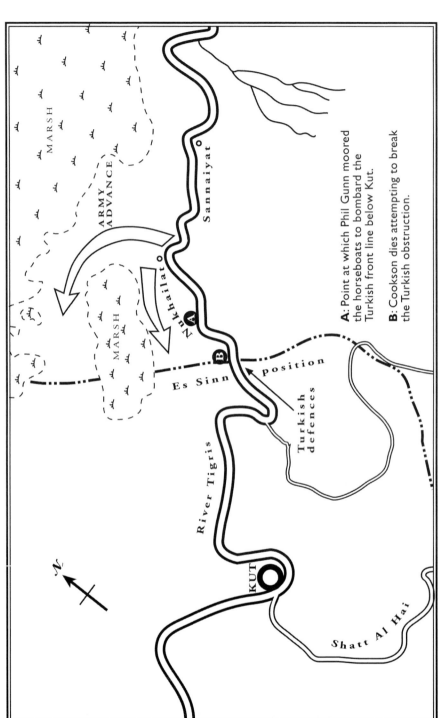

The Battle of Es Sinn, which led to the capture of Kut al Amara.

A: Point at which Phil Gunn moored the horseboats to bombard the Turkish front line below Kut.

B: Cookson dies attempting to break the Turkish obstruction.

MARSH

ARMY ADVANCE

Sannaiyat

Nukhailat

MARSH

Es Sinn position

Turkish defences

River Tigris

KUT

Shatt Al Hai

N

and attack the Turks from their left wing and behind. As they marched away Phil could not help noticing that their equipment was carried on an assortment of camels, bullocks and donkeys. He had heard that the army was short of transport and were obviously scraping the barrel.

* * *

At about 5.00 am the following morning, an army officer, smartly dressed in tropical helmet and khaki, came aboard, roused Phil and asked him his name. Wanted to make sure he had come to the right boat, he said, and introduced himself as the forward observing officer – FOO for short. It was his job, he explained, to assess where the horse boats' guns' shells should be aimed. He would embark in RN2 and they would go upriver in support of our advancing army. When they had reached suitable positions he would instruct Phil to moor the horse boats alongside the bank where it was low enough for the guns to fire over it. Phil was to rig the ladder with which the launch was equipped vertically above it. Up this would climb the FOO, with his binoculars, to control the firing of the guns (see illustration). He instructed Phil to raise steam, collect the horse boats and proceed upriver.

Phil, adrenalin running at the prospect of action, shook his crew. The FOO went to brief the gun crews in the two horse boats moored to the bank astern of the launch. They were already preparing ammunition by the time steam had been raised for Phil to manoeuvre RN2 out and secure the two boats alongside. He got them out into the river, where he handed over to his Indian coxswain to steer upstream.

Phil looked over at the soldiers on the right-hand side preparing to advance and in his launch, towing the horse boats, they steamed with them.

'Which regiment are they Sir?' he enquired of the officer, whose name, he discovered, was Lieutenant Johnston of the Royal Artillery.

'I think it's the Norfolks, an Indian regiment – the 7th Rajputs – and some Dorsets,' was the reply.

The fact that they were getting close to the enemy was indicated by a shell that whistled over their heads. Phil instinctively ducked and the officer laughed.

'We're going to have plenty of those,' he said. 'But hopefully we're going to give the Turks a hell of a lot more than they give us. Rig up the spotting ladder.'

Phil ordered his crew to lash the ladder vertically up alongside the cabin of RN2. He had rigged it with a small platform and steadying post at the top to help the observing officer keep his balance. He hoped the Turks wouldn't shoot it down, exposed as it was.

'Now I want you to take the boats into the right bank another 100 yards upriver and moor them as close in as you can,' ordered Johnston. 'Pick a spot clear of palm trees so that I can see what is happening out on the battlefield and the fire from the guns is not obstructed.'

Phil passed orders to the coxswain and stayed close to the Indian to supervise the positioning of the launch.

'Stand by to cast off the starboard horse boat,' he ordered his crewmen, who immediately manned the lines to that boat and took some turns of rope off the bollards that secured it. 'We're going to put you alongside here,' he called to the seamen in the boat. 'If you take your lines ashore to secure your starboard side I'll lay out anchors in the stream to steady you to port.'

They had practised the manoeuvre well and on its completion positioned the second horse boat close to the first. Horse boat seamen adjusted the lines, securing them to the shore so that they both lay at the same angle. This would make the gunnery direction task of the forward observing officer easier. Phil anchored the launch just offshore between the two horse boats.

At this point the right-hand riverbank against which the horse boats were moored was quite low. It was easy to see over it but the river was also narrower than had recently been the case. On the other side Phil could see the tops of some palm trees behind a relatively high riverbank that hid view of the ground beyond it.

Horse boats secured, Lieutenant Johnston climbed up the ladder that had been prepared for him and took out his binoculars from their leather case, bleached to a yellow by the burning sun to which it had been subjected. Phil looked out across the plain to the right and in the distance upriver found he could just distinguish some long, low mounds that were obviously the Turkish front line trenches. In a downriver direction he could see a line of British and Indian infantry advancing towards them. Johnston had mentioned that some of the Dorset Regiment were there and he wondered if Knocker, his friend from home, was among them.

Chapter 34

Death of a Friend

I t suddenly became evident to Phil that they were ahead of the IEF front line and, therefore, there was nothing in between his launch, the horse boats and the enemy. He felt he ought to raise this point with the officer but it was too late as Johnston was already up the ladder with his binoculars trained on the Turks ahead and out to the right.

Johnston turned to look at the horse boats to check the direction in which they were lying. He would have to give them orders in relation to this – green to starboard (right) and red to port (left). They had no compasses and only a spirit level to determine the angle of the guns, with a printed table to indicate what angle would result in what range.

'Train to green 30 degrees!' he called to the gun crews in both horse boats. 'Lay to 3,000 yards!'

'Load!'

The gun crews loaded their 4.7-inch projectiles into the breeches of the guns, which were then slammed shut and a handle turned to seal them.

'Ready to fire Sir!' came successively from each of them.

'Shoot!'

Two monumental bangs occurred almost simultaneously as each gun fired, followed by a whistling sound as the projectiles tore away towards their target. Phil, who had been involved in gunnery shoots in *Clio* before, nevertheless thought his eardrums would burst. Too late he remembered the ear plugs with which he and his Indian crew had been issued and hastily went to tell them, seeking out and donning his own. The forward observing officer watched the fall of shot closely through his binoculars.

'Stand by for corrections! Train to green 32. Lay to 3,200 yards! Shoot when ready!

The guns crews, who had already loaded in anticipation, made the necessary adjustments and a further two shells whistled off towards the Turkish lines.

But it was not to be all one-sided. In a very few minutes shells were coming in their direction from the Turks. The first were well over, the next few equally short, but then they started to land close by, raising splashes from the river and showers of sand from the land. Phil noticed that those that landed ashore threw up clods of damp sand and that from a few yards in from the bank marsh grass appeared to be growing. He also noticed that a body of about 100 IEF soldiers was marching parallel to the bank and about 50 yards in from it. They would be marching into the marshy area. He wondered whether he should warn them but they were soldiers and must know what they were doing. Suddenly the Turkish shelling stopped, which was a relief.

The marching British soldiers were now close enough for him to recognize from their shoulder badges that they were in fact the Dorsets, the regiment of his chum Knocker White. But then a disturbing thing happened. The first of them came up to the marsh grass and he could see that they were sinking into the ground. Similarly he had sunk into the mud off Borneo, only saved from being sucked under by Lieutenant Commander Cookson's timely order to fall forward. The first half-dozen ranks were starting to sink when the sergeant in charge clearly realized what was happening and must have ordered them to halt and turn about. Those at the back did just that, dragging their feet in the mud initially and then marching in step out of danger. Their colleagues in front were not so lucky. It was obviously some kind of quicksand and they continued to sink down into the boggy ground. The sergeant halted his squad and came back to take charge of those in trouble.

Phil wondered whether Knocker had the misfortune to be among those, but at that moment Johnston descended the ladder during a break in the action.

'Mind if I borrow your glasses for a moment Sir?' asked Phil. 'The Dorsets seem to be in trouble over there.'

'Yes, I saw that. Doubtless their sergeant will get them out of it. Not at all Gunn. Help yourself.' He handed the binoculars over.

Phil focused them on the floundering soldiers, identifying the face of each but hoping Knocker wouldn't be one of them. His hope was not fulfilled for there, in the rank nearest the river, was the unmistakeable face of his fellow former pupil from Hampton Wick Church Elementary School. Knocker, like his colleagues, was struggling to escape from the muddy sand into which they all appeared to be sinking.

Ordinary Seaman Phillip Gunn in tropical uniform, Hong Kong, 1914. (*Author's copyright*)

On seeing her for the first time, Phil Gunn thought HMS *Clio* looked like a rich man's magnificent steam yacht. But her six 4-inch calibre guns could hit hard and accurately. (*Author's copyright*)

HMS *Clio's* drum and fife band. Phil Gunn, standing third from left, found his fife less heavy than a rifle as the band accompanied the route marches ashore on the way to Mesopotamia. (*Author's copyright*)

The Royal Marine butcher would kill one of the cattle when required, the distressed beast being pulled unwillingly with ropes by the duty watch of seamen towards a chute. It would then be poleaxed with a sledgehammer, the carcase cut up and the blood, offal and other unwanted parts discharged into the sea through the chute, which was designed to keep the ship's side clean.

Meals were prepared by the sailors themselves on their own mess tables and taken to the galley, where the one qualified cook in the ship heated them. Over and around these same mess tables they would sling their hammocks in which to sleep at night.

HMS *Clio* had no power-driven appliances so everything had to be done by hand, including weighing anchor. This was sometimes necessary a number of times a day, in all depths of water and often out of a muddy bottom from which the anchor had to be 'broken'. It needed sixteen brawny seamen pushing with their chests against wooden bars to turn the capstan in order to do this.

Coaling ship to provide fuel for HMS *Clio's* boilers was done by securing a lighter alongside the ship and sending hands down into it who shovelled the coal into sacks. These were then hoisted inboard by a derrick and the coal tipped down holes in the deck into the ship's bunkers. The whole ship's company, dressed in their oldest clothes, took part in this very dirty operation.

When no derrick was available to bring the coal inboard, it was necessary to rig stages and pass it up from the lighter in baskets – a very laborious task.

Phillip Gunn 1974

Clio had three tall wooden masts whose safety was sometimes threatened by typhoons. To avoid possible whipping and snapping of the upper two masts in these conditions they would be lowered and fixed to the more substantial lower mast. This was often practised, as in this painting, so that it could be done quickly.

Continuous steaming in tropical heat resulted in some of the stokers collapsing so that seamen volunteers were called for to relieve them. Phil Gunn was among them and found himself down in the boiler room with a shovel, gasping for breath in the intense heat when the furnace doors were opened to allow more coal to be shovelled through them. He subsequently retained considerable respect for stokers in coal-burning ships.

Shore leave was taken when possible and here sailors from *Clio* are landing in white suits with straw hats normally worn on Sundays and in a tropical climate. They had no suitcases but carried their possessions ashore in large, strong blue handkerchiefs with which they had been issued for this purpose.

Clio had no lookout position as she had been designed to work up the rivers of China, where sea warfare was not envisaged. Now, in the open seas and operating against German shipping, they needed one and lashed a rum barrel up the foremast in which the lookouts would sit for two-hour watches. Phil sang every song he could remember to offset the discomfort that resulted.

Four seamen were needed to control *Clio's* large wheel for steering her in choppy water, particularly when tributaries flowed into narrow rivers with strong currents. These steersmen could not see the ship's progress and an officer's wheel orders reached them through a voice pipe from the bridge above.

The Turks, guided by German officers, were floating mines down the Tigris with the aim of sinking the Royal Navy's advancing ships. The sailors in the sloops moored in the river at Qurna used ropes and spars to rig mine catchers across their ships' bows. These prevented contact with the ships' sides, none of which was damaged.

Out from the starboard side of the sloops and around their sterns swarmed a mass of *bellums* (canoes), lashed in pairs and with their occupants protected against fire from the fort they were assaulting by steel shields fixed across their bows. Paddled by soldiers of the Oxfordshire and Buckinghamshire Light Infantry they tore towards the beach while the sloops bombarded the enemy positions with their guns. The advance up the Tigris had begun.

BELLUMS (CANOES) AS USED TO STORM THE INITIAL TURKISH STRONGHOLD OF THE MESOPOTAMIA CAMPAIGN - 1915/16

H

A Turkish gunboat, driven ashore and destroyed by the gunfire of HM ships *Clio* and *Espiegle*, north of Qurna. (*Author's copyright*)

The Army advanced in their stern-wheel paddle steamers, securing to the bank in the evening as it was impossible to navigate the fast-flowing, uncharted river at night.

Phil was selected to take charge of a former Calcutta River police launch towing two horse boats from the Suez Canal, each with a 4.7-inch gun believed to have last been used during the Boer War in 1899. They were to bombard the Turks in support of the advancing Army, their fire controlled by an Army spotting officer up a ladder that Phil lashed vertically for him.

Phil Gunn received two unexpected items in 1915. There was the handsome brass box full of pipe tobacco from Princess Mary's Gift Fund. Less welcome was the enemy bullet he found in his pillow when waking up on the deck of launch RN2 up the river Tigris. (*Author's copyright*)

Captured Turkish soldiers under armed guard by the river Tigris with a Royal Navy sloop steaming past. (*Copyright: JJ Heath-Caldwell*)

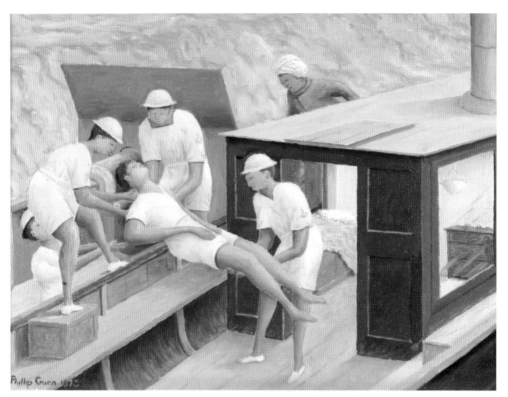

The force had captured Amara, Kut al Amara, and was engaged in the Battle of Ctesiphon just short of Baghdad when Phil collapsed with severe malaria. He had contracted it from continuous, vicious mosquito bites suffered as they advanced up the Tigris. Phil was carried ashore unconscious by his shipmates and laid on the bank.

During the retreat from Ctesiphon, and after he was carried ashore unconscious, Phil's launch was sunk by enemy fire. Its entire crew were killed.

Note: Phillip Gunn painted all the colour pictures shown here. The author owns the copyright to reproduce them.

There was nothing Phil could do at this distance. A gleam of hope came when it appeared that a small number of the thirty or so soldiers managed to struggle free. They were those who had the presence of mind to do exactly what Phil had been told to do off Borneo – fall forward so that their bodies were flat. Other soldiers from among those who had escaped the quagmire, and the sergeant, were doing their best to extricate their colleagues. These were conditions to which they were clearly not used.

'Fall flat and crawl out Knocker,' he shouted ineffectually, as his friend was much too far away to hear his voice. Knocker White seemed to be a few yards away from the rest of the group.

Then something, he never knew what, made Phil look away from the scene across the river to the raised bank on the other side. A small movement and a metallic glint in the leaves of a palm tree caught his eye. Phil strained to identify what it was that he was seeing. The obvious barrel of a rifle peered slowly out from between the leaves. It was levelled at the struggling soldiers across the river.

Phil dashed to get his own rifle. It must be a Turkish sniper up in the palm. His hands could hardly work fast enough to find his ammunition and rapidly load the .303. He came out of the cabin, knelt and took careful aim at the point from which the barrel appeared from the palm and pulled the trigger.

But just before he did so came the unmistakeable crack of the 7.65mm German Mauser rifle, with which the Turkish infantry was equipped.

'Good God! What are you up to?' enquired the observing officer.

There was a pause of a few seconds. Then a uniformed body and a rifle tumbled separately out of the tree and fell to the ground.

'Well done lad!' congratulated Johnston. 'Didn't know he was there.'

But Phil was already focusing on the group of struggling soldiers, nearly all of whom had now managed to free themselves from the quicksand that had trapped them. All, that is, except one, which, to his horror, was Knocker. His face was now barely above the level of the soft ground and lay over at an angle. It was white even with the tan they all had from the unforgiving sun of the Mesopotamian summer. As it sank down to rest on the ground Phil could see Knocker mouthing something. He would never know what. Through the middle of his temple was a hole through which blood was gently trickling.

It wasn't the first dead or dying body Phil had seen. He had seen plenty floating down the river Tigris, killed in the various battles the army had been fighting. Chinese rivers, too, had seemed to have their fair share of floating corpses, while in colonies of sampans at places like Canton, cries in the night frequently meant that someone had fallen overboard and, as few of them could swim, that was usually the end of whoever it was. Sailors used to say with macabre humour that it helped the fishing out there by providing fish with plenty of food.

But this was different. This was someone he had known since they were seven years old. It was like losing a brother that he had only just caught up with again.

Chapter 35

A Gun Battle

There was no time for mourning.

'Stand by the guns,' ordered Lieutenant Johnston, who had been watching morse signals by the light of a distant lamp. 'We're going to have a long shoot.'

Grabbing his binoculars from Phil he jumped over to the vertical ladder, shinned up it and focused on the Turkish trenches, which were about a mile and a half away across the desert. Phil put his earplugs in and told his crew to do the same.

And so, for about an hour, the 4.7-inch guns carried out a continuous bombardment of the Turks. It was to soften them up preparatory to our troops advancing, explained Johnston. Regularly he would alter the bearing and elevation of the guns to concentrate the fire where it was most effective.

It was not long before the Turks replied and a series of shells started to land and explode near the launch and horse boats, gradually getting ever nearer.

'Time to move I think,' called the observing officer when one landed so close that the splashes from the river soaked the launch.

Phil ordered the engine, for which steam had been kept at a low level for such an eventuality, to be brought to life. They weighed anchor and, taking the horse boats in tow, moved further downriver to a different position a few hundred yards away to spoil the Turkish gunners' aim. It seemed to work as the enemy shells continued to land where they had been before. Bombardment of the Turks recommenced but it would only be a matter of time before their new position would be found. Every now and again Lieutenant Johnston called on the gun crews to open fire on the Turkish forces. These were some distance away and now difficult to discern in the heat haze.

During the whole operation Phil, .303 rifle at the ready, kept as much of a watch as he could on the palms and high bank on the other side of the river. He got his crew to do the same to try and detect any of the sniper activity that had killed Knocker White, but there was none.

'Cease fire!' Eventually the order came from the observing officer, who then descended his ladder.

It was not an able seaman's job to know what tactics were being used to defeat the Turks in the taking of Kut. But Phil was curious and Johnston sufficiently friendly for him to feel he could enquire.

'That's the main Turkish front line we're bombarding extending out to the right of the river,' the officer explained. 'It goes out to a marsh. Our troops on the left side crossed the river after dark and joined those on the right to make a large force. Overnight this force should go beyond the marsh, turn round it, and attack the enemy from the far side and rear where they will be least expecting it. The purpose of our bombardment here is to make them think this – in front of them on both sides of the river is where our main attack will be coming from.'

'What about the other side of the river Sir – over on the left?' asked Phil.

'Quite clever really,' said the officer, 'or it will be if it comes off.' He went on to explain that the army had made a lot of noise and menacing moves over beyond the left bank, which would tie up a lot of Turks to maintain a big defence there to counter it. He drew Phil's attention to the fact that every now and again he had been directing some of the firing over onto the left bank, the object being to try and make the Turks even more convinced that this would be followed up by an infantry attack on that side. There was also the frontal attack they had been witnessing on the right bank. In reality the main attack would be between two marshes well out to the right and then round on the Turks' left flank.

Johnston went on to explain that the marshy ground in which Knocker White and his fellows had become trapped was a small and unexpected area. They had few reliable maps and this sort of tragedy was inevitable.

Chapter 36

Reflection but Still no Recognition

There seemed to be a pause in activity. Phil went to the edge of the launch and sat down to contemplate the welcome peace of the river, reeds growing along its opposite bank. A small water bird emerged, apparently oblivious that part of a world war was taking place within sight. It swam purposefully about seeking insects to grab with its businesslike beak and then retired into the reeds again.

Phil's mind dwelt sadly on Knocker. Memories arose how they, and other boys from school, used to go into the sports ground near the Thames to play football on a Saturday morning. The thought reminded him of home. It was about 11 o'clock in the morning and his mother would be doing some washing out in the scullery at the back.... She might have got on to squeezing the water out between the wooden rollers of the large mangle, which she operated by winding the metal wheel that turned them. Then she would hang it on the line in the back garden, propping up the centre with a forked stick so that the clothes hung well clear of the ground.

His father sometimes read the *Daily Mail* and had sent out a copy a little while back dated 5 April 1915, which was Phil's birthday. There was a new cartoon strip called 'Teddy Tail of the *Daily Mail*' about a half-boy, half-mouse who had a knot in his tail. Phil decided he preferred his favourite, Billy Bunter. By the time it got to him at Basra the paper was months old but its other content had caused Phil to ponder.

There was massive and detailed coverage of what was going on in the trenches in France and also mention of a terrible naval battle called Coronel in the Pacific Ocean that had taken place some time before in November 1914. It had been the first defeat of the Royal Navy in a naval action since before the Battle of Trafalgar and the navy had lost 1,600 men. Phil was shocked at this: he was part of a navy that didn't get beaten. But there was still not a single mention of what our forces in Mesopotamia were doing.

The same issue was still troubling people back in Britain. On 21 September 1915, Colonel Yate MP asked the Secretary of State for India, Mr Austen Chamberlain, when the dispatches relating to the operations in Mesopotamia would be published in the *London Gazette*.

On 22 September, *The Times* pointed out:

Of all the campaigns now in progress that in Mesopotamia is the only one in which the Allies can claim continual success. It is as much a British war as the campaign in Flanders. Thousands of Englishmen are engaged in it. Steps should be taken without delay to ensure that future dispatches receive ample circulation in Great Britain.

On the same day, Sir John Rees MP rose to speak in the House of Commons:

The campaign in Mesopotamia is the most uniformly successful yet waged by our army and navy, and yet one about which it seems very difficult to get any information: I do not think that in this country the enormous difficulties under which our troops and sailors have operated in the Persian Gulf and up the Tigris are appreciated. The heat during July and August is intense. I have myself seen it up to 133 degrees [56°C] in the shade. The inhabitants never venture out of doors. In the capital city of Baghdad they spend the days in the cellar and sleep at night on the roof. Yet it is in this possibly most trying climate in the world that our troops and sailors have maintained a gallant fight and have won victories. It is disappointing to me that we have not heard more about it here so that the country might legitimately rejoice in the extremely gallant exploits of this force which has had to contend, not only with brave enemies in the Turks and also with the Arabs, but with many other difficulties. I do not suggest that the gallant troops and sailors are concerned, but people in this country are anxious about the matter and would like due honour to be done to their gallant and successful actions. I dare say the House will be aware that this expedition is fitted out from India and the dispatches are sent to that government. I suppose that is one of the reasons why in this country we hear so little about it. It is a British campaign, just as much as any other. More information should be forthcoming concerning the operations in Mesopotamia and that portion of our military operations should not be left out of sight as has hitherto been the case. Naval interests are also very much affected because this expedition is engaged in protecting the oil pipeline for which this country lately paid some £2,000,000 for the supply of oil on which the navy is so dependent.

Chapter 37

Ordered Forward to Destroy a River Obstacle

Back on the Tigris Phil's Indian coxswain came over to him and exclaimed excitedly, 'Troops advancing, Able Seaman Phil!'

He stood up and looked across the desert. Sure enough, groups of infantry were moving across the plain towards the Turkish front line but after a while they stopped. Spades were produced and they dug trenches, throwing up the earth in front of them across a wide front.

As the heat of the day bore down upon the scene, gradually and mysteriously the digging troops disappeared and all Phil could see was the desert and the sky above it. The Turkish front line, which had been clearly visible, also shimmered and faded from sight.

'Not quite sure what's happened Sir,' Phil remarked to Johnston, who had returned after a brief visit to headquarters downriver. 'I could see our troops digging their trenches and the enemy beyond, and then they just vanished.'

'You've been caught by the mirage again, Gunn. It's a damned nuisance and makes my job a lot harder. Believe me, they're still digging themselves in in front of the enemy trenches. As I said, we want the Turks to think they are going to be attacked from the front here. In fact, our main attack is the large force we have going round beyond the marshes to get at them from the Turkish flank.'

Late in the afternoon a trooper from the cavalry galloped up and pulled his horse to a halt alongside the launch. Lieutenant Johnston, realizing this was probably a message for him, went ashore and was handed an envelope with a smart salute. The trooper mounted and galloped off in the direction from whence he had come. Johnston opened the envelope and read its contents, which consisted of a single sheet of paper.

He stuffed it into his pocket and clambered back aboard the launch, calling the leading seamen gunners of Phil's two horse boats over.

'The Turks have laid an obstacle across the river a mile or so on at a place called Es Sinn, more or less in line with their trenches out to either side,' said Johnston, addressing the leading seamen and Phil.

'The general has asked if we can get rid of it so I want you to take your horse boats up, position them where I tell you, and your guns are to bombard the obstruction. I gather it consists of a *mahaila*, one of those big dhow-like river craft, and two iron lighters, all joined together by wire hawsers.

'Anyhow, we want to blow it away so that the navy can continue the advance upstream in support of the army. Get cracking then. I will work out where to moor alongside the bank.'

One of the leading seamen acknowledged the order with an 'Aye aye Sir' to Johnston, whose surprise Phil noted as the army officer was clearly not used to such nautical forms of address.

The horse boat leading seamen jumped ashore. Phil got the launch under way and manoeuvred it to collect their two unpowered vessels, which had been re-supplied with ammunition from a barge during the recent wait. His crewmen lashed the horse boats alongside. Phil worked the clumsy trio to face upstream and handed over to his coxswain as they chugged up the river.

After about fifteen minutes Lieutenant Johnston got up onto the canopy of the launch's cabin and looked ahead with his binoculars. They were approaching a right-hand bend in the river and as they came to it he jumped down and ordered Phil to put the horse boats in against the left-hand bank.

Phil suddenly became aware that they were now well ahead of the front line and was concerned that they might run into enemy troops or snipers, unprotected as they appeared to be. While going about his work he asked Johnston what was between them and the Turks. The forward observing officer pointed out that the IEF did have advance parties of troops ahead either side of the river but they were concealed in drainage ditches.

Phil positioned the horse boats alongside the bank with anchors laid out in the stream to steady them for bombardment. He secured the launch alongside and, his work done, picked up his binoculars and looked ahead up the river. A straight stretch went some distance away from the bend on which they were moored. Sure enough, there across the Tigris were three vessels, two of them iron barges, and in between those the *mahaila*, linked together with strong wire hawsers that collectively provided a complete barrier to anything larger than a rowing boat proceeding beyond it.

The sun was starting to drop through the leaves of the palm trees that lined the river and the FOO wished to make maximum use of the failing light. 'Stand by the guns!' he ordered. 'Lay to 1,200 yards, train to green one zero. Load at will.'

The layers and trainers in the gun crews brought their weapons to bear as Johnston had ordered. The rest of the crew loaded the projectiles into the breeches and stood by with more.

'Ready?'

'Ready Sir!'

'Shoot!'

Phil had had no need to tell his Indian crewmen to don their earplugs this time. They were now used to taking the precautionary measure to avoid the effects of the loud bangs made by the 4.7s.

Two shells went off, leaving their customary whistling sound behind and creating splashes just beyond the obstruction that was their target. Johnston brought down the angle of the guns a shade to reduce the range, made a minor adjustment to the direction and a further two projectiles left the horse boats.

And so the bombardment went on.

They hit the iron barges and the *mahaila* repeatedly but although they could see the shudder and rocking of the vessels as the shells exploded on impact with them, they still stayed afloat.

'We need to hit them on the waterline or break the hawsers,' muttered Johnston, frustrated. He ordered a further reduction in elevation and the guns went on.

But it was no good. The obstruction remained in place despite the rocking of the vessels with the constant impact of the shells. The FOO ordered the ceasefire and left to report to headquarters. In the launch and horse boats they brewed cups of tea and awaited further orders.

Chapter 38

A Victoria Cross

About half an hour afterwards a strange thing happened. It might have been a movement in the corner of his eye but something made Phil look downriver. In the gloom he detected the shapes of an armed paddle steamer and two tugs of the naval flotilla, all lights out, creeping upstream. They passed the launch, the now silent horse boats, and steamed quietly up towards the obstruction, right between the trenches of the Turkish Army that extended out to right and left. Phil watched in amazed anticipation.

As they neared the obstruction, the Turks discovered their presence and a barrage of heavy rifle and machine-gun fire poured onto them from either side. Phil winced as he saw the paddles of the armed steamer churn up the water to increase speed and head straight for the *mahaila* in the middle of the river. It rammed the vessel, clearly in the hope of sinking it, but the Arab craft remained afloat. The steamer then went alongside the *mahaila*. In the light created by the gun and rifle flashes Phil witnessed a familiar tall figure in white naval officer's uniform, large axe in hand, leap down onto it and hack away at the lashings that held the wire hawsers. Cookson could not have wielded more than five or six strokes before he appeared to stiffen and then fall under the rattle of rifle fire from the banks, collapsing onto the deck of the *mahaila*. The crew of the steamer, some wounded, retrieved his body.

Phil, numbed, saw the three vessels still under heavy fire turn in the river and come downstream towards them. Having made their turn the Turkish gunfire suddenly appeared redirected towards Phil's RN2. Rifle bullets started to splash into the water around them, over their heads and into the boat's structure. As the returning vessels came abreast the launch a figure emerged onto the wing of the bridge of Cookson's steamer and shouted to him through a megaphone. In the darkness Phil was unable to see the devastating damage that *Comet* had sustained from the withering Turkish rifle fire now coming his way as well.

'Lieutenant Harris here. Pick up the horse boats and follow us downstream. We're going to anchor for the night at Nukhailat a mile or so down, where we'll be behind our front line.'

'Aye aye Sir!' replied Phil.

'I'm afraid the senior naval officer, Lieutenant Commander Cookson, was killed.'

'Yes Sir. We saw.'

They cast off the launch and, still under heavy fire, Phil manoeuvred her to go alongside each horse boat in turn. With the aid of their crews he took them in tow and headed downstream and out of range of the hail of bullets. He still could not understand why neither he nor his crew had been hit because he could see bullet holes all over RN2.

The figure that had leapt over onto the *mahaila* was unmistakeably the man who had rescued him from the mud in Borneo, 'made one' with the sailors in *Clio's* football team and taken charge of evolutions on board. Initially it was he who should have commanded RN2 but he had been big enough to put his trust in a young able seaman to do the job. In life, Cookson[1] had been a hero to Phil, who had now seen him die the death of a hero.

Note

1. Lieutenant Commander Edgar Cookson RN, who had already won the Distinguished Service Order for bravery in Mesopotamia, was now posthumously awarded the Victoria Cross for his action at Es Sinn. Able Seaman Phillip Gunn, twenty, was awarded the Distinguished Service Medal for his 'command and handling of HM Launch RN2 and for good work in towing the horse boats under fire'.

Chapter 39

Horror After the Battle

O ut in the desert dramatic things were happening. Major General Townshend's battle plan had been brilliantly successful. His troops had attacked the Turks from their left flank as planned and driven them down towards the Tigris, where the survivors escaped back along the river towards Kut.

The medical services had not yet got to the scene after the battle and, inevitably in the dark, wounded troops lay out on the ground unable to move. Into this scene crept Arabs who had been waiting on the sidelines to glean any pickings that were left for them by the principal combatant armies. Both Turks and British were invaders of their tribally oriented and often merciless land. They had no allegiance to either so would take what they could.

They moved stealthily among the bodies lying on the battlefield, removing and spiriting away clothing and weapons from the dead. When they came across a wounded soldier it was the work of a moment to whip out a curved dagger and cut his throat. They would then pull any gold from his teeth and steal his possessions.

The more brutally disposed gouged out the eyes of helpless men before leaving them alive but disfigured and in despair on the ground. A few of the British troops travelling back across the battlefield caught three Arabs in the act of brutalizing one of their fellow soldiers. They swiftly erected a gallows, hanged them and left them to swing in the night air.

* * *

Oblivious to the details of what was going on ashore, Phil woke up at dawn the following morning wondering what the day would bring. Would it be as eventful as the preceding day? Would he still be alive at the end of it?

His crew breakfasted and then cleaned the launch. He exchanged thoughts with the seamen in the horse boats.

They did not have long to wait. An army officer cantered up on horseback at about 8.00 am and shouted across to them. The Turks were in full retreat beyond Kut, he told them. The IEF was going to pursue the enemy. Phil, towing the horse boats, was to go on to Kut.

Phil asked him how they were to get past the obstruction that had been preventing their advance the night before. That was now gone, he was told.

They cast off from the bank, secured the horse boats alongside and RN2 steamed on upstream. They passed the fateful point at which Cookson had met his death, now deserted by the Turks who had appeared so menacing the night before. Eight miles further on, they went alongside in Kut al Amara.

* * *

Back in the House of Commons on 29 September 1915, the Secretary of State for India rose to speak.

'I have received two telegrams, both dated 29 September, from Sir John Nixon, which I will read to the House.'

'The first telegram says:

Complete success attended the operations on the Tigris on 28 September. The position of the enemy is a long one on both banks astride the river, 7 miles to the East of Kut and extending from the right* bank for 6 miles. The plan of attack was well conceived. General Delamain's detached force consisting of two brigades, after a demonstration which they made on 27 September, crossed over from the left* bank. By a night march they gained the enemy's left, and by a gallant attack carried its northern extremity at 10.00 am. By 2.00 pm the remainder of this portion of the enemy's position was carried after much opposition. By nightfall the force had advanced west of the enemy's position, which was wired in and strongly entrenched and in which the enemy had been pinned all

---

* As previously stated, for ease of understanding 'right' indicates the bank on the right as seen from the advancing vessels, and 'left' to that on their left throughout this book.

day by another brigade. The troops bivouacked in their position with the fall of darkness, our outer flank was covered by armoured motor cars and cavalry, which were engaged all day against Turkish cavalry. The Turks had to be dislodged trench by trench and fought with the greatest tenacity. Some guns and several hundred prisoners, with many rifles and quantities of ammunition, were captured, and the enemy's losses in dead were very severe, the trenches being full of corpses. It is believed that our casualties are under 500.

'The other telegram says "Enemy position in advance of Kut al Amara captured with many prisoners and guns. Enemy in full flight towards Baghdad. Our force pushing in pursuit".'

Nixon's telegrams made no mention of the wounded who had lain out overnight in the wake of the British advance, some of whom Arabs from nearby tribes had robbed, mutilated and murdered. The medical arrangements had broken down and wounded who could walk had sometimes wandered around for hours before receiving attention. Hot by day, the November night was bitterly cold and others died from this and sheer exhaustion.

The armed tugs had forged ahead above Kut and attacked two Turkish steamers that were carrying both escaping soldiers and ammunition, some of which they captured. The British vessels found navigation difficult in view of the low level of the poorly charted river. Two of them ran aground before freeing themselves and returning to Kut, where Major General Townshend was now installed to plan the next part of the campaign. Fortunately, running aground in a vessel driven by side paddles was not as serious as it might have been with propellers under the hull, but you still had to get afloat again. After such a rapid advance, the army also needed to consolidate and make sure its supplies were adequate before proceeding further.

Chapter 40

Phil to Work for Townshend

Phil was supervising the taking of some stores aboard RN2 when he saw Lieutenant Harris walk down the jetty towards the launch, which he then clambered aboard. Lieutenant Harris had called across to him the news of Cookson's death the night before and was now temporarily senior naval officer.

Bearing in mind the seriousness of the campaign and the major part the Royal Navy was playing in fighting in ships through the desert, Phil found himself surprised that the SNO was now only a lieutenant RN. The original SNO had been the captain of HMS *Espiegle*, equivalent to a full colonel in the army, but he was nowhere in the vicinity. In his place had been Lieutenant Commander Cookson, but he had been killed. So this heavy responsibility now rested on a relatively lowly lieutenant.

Phil saluted and the young SNO enquired about the condition of RN2 and its crew after its adventures of the previous day. He was able to assure Harris that all was well in the craft.

Harris then raised the problems of feeding the launch's crew with army-slaughtered meat, about which he had heard. Phil was able to assure him that although the crew had wanted their meat killed by the halal method, he had sorted it out in the end.

'As you know, the army is on both sides of the river here. Major General Townshend needs to be able to get back and forth across it so I have allocated you and RN2 to him and his staff for that. You'd better go and report to his ADC[1] and do whatever they want. You can leave the horse boats here with their crews. Give them a chance to re-ammunition. They won't be needed until we continue the advance and that won't be for a bit. Is all that clear?'

'Yes Sir, I'll do it right away.'

Phil tidied himself up. He scrubbed the white canvas gym shoes that sailors wore for boat work and changed into the spare white shirt and shorts that he had recently washed in the murky waters of the Tigris. He set out along the jetty to find the general's headquarters, which was in a building near the waterfront.

* * *

The ADC was an immaculately dressed army captain, smelling of eau de cologne and seated behind a desk. Phil explained who he was and why he had come. The ADC told Phil to sit down outside the office of the general, who was seeing a senior cavalry officer. Phil could not help overhearing the conversation the other side of the fly curtain that hung in the intervening doorway.

'But why couldn't you pursue the enemy?' asked the general. 'They were well on the run?'

'Well Sir, my Sikh and Hindu cavalry had had a hard day helping to win the battle that drove the Turks to leave Kut. They needed to eat and we had food. But owing to lack of transport we were unable to bring their cooking pots and they will not use the Arab cooking pots found in the villages to prepare their food.'

'Good God!' said Townshend angrily. 'Lack of transport on land and water is one of the problems of this campaign. Now, evidently, so is lack of cooking pots. This means we have given them the chance to regroup, which I was trying to avoid.' Then, wearily, 'All right.'

The cavalry officer emerged through the fly curtain. The ADC rose to his feet, accompanied by that wave of eau de cologne, showed him out and turned to Phil.

'I'll take you in to see the general,' he said coldly, vanishing through the curtain before re-emerging to beckon Phil through.

Phil put his uniform cap on, walked through the door, stood to attention in front of the general's desk and saluted. Townshend looked up from his papers. The ADC retired.

'What's your name?'

'Able Seaman Gunn Sir, launch RN2.'

General Townshend's eyes narrowed. 'Haven't I seen you before?'

'Yes Sir, in the *Comet*, when you were there. I was transferred to the *Shaitan* on the way to Amara.'

'I wish all operations went as smoothly as that one did,' commented the general drily.

'Right, Gunn, well we're going to need you and your launch. I and my staff have to get back and forth across the Tigris here at Kut and, as you will have seen, there is no bridge. So the senior naval officer has kindly said you can ferry us when we need to cross.'

'Yes Sir.'

'I want you to moor alongside the bank opposite my headquarters here and we'll tell you when we need you and where we want to get to. Off you go.'

Townshend returned to his deliberations on the desk, opening a book that Phil could see was about Napoleon. He saluted, turned about and marched out of the office. Phil stopped at the desk of the ADC, not sure whether he should say anything to him. The ADC continued his paperwork and without looking up said, 'You heard what the general said – "Off you go".'

Phil marched out of the building and walked in more relaxed fashion back to RN2, which was about 500 yards downstream. He pondered on the difference in attitude towards him of the two officers he had just encountered. The general, although formal, had certainly been more welcoming than the ADC but that was what he had noticed about life. The people at the top didn't feel they had to make their superiority felt like the people on the way up.

Note
1. Aide-de-camp (French). An officer on a general's staff who assists him in routine matters.

Chapter 41

Collecting Canoes for a Bridge

Phil moved RN2 round and secured opposite the army headquarters. For the next day or so he and his Indian crew took the general, ADC and other army staff officers across and up and down the river at Kut as they required.

'We are now just a ferry, Able Seaman Phil,' observed his Indian coxswain, quite happy to be out of the firing line.

'Yes, but I don't suppose that will last long,' replied Phil.

Phil was not really certain what was going on. He knew that opposite Kut the shallow Shatt al Hai River connected the Tigris to the Euphrates via about 140 miles of desert. He had heard that this was why they had taken Kut, to oversee the entrance to the Hai and prevent the Turks moving from one of the great rivers to the other. However, now there was talk of driving the Turks well beyond Kut and even trying to capture the capital, Baghdad. It had been difficult for the navy to follow up the rout of the Turks after the Battle of Kut because it was now September and the level of the river Tigris was falling fast, as it always did in the second half of the year. So vessels were running aground in this poorly charted river and the possibility of hot pursuit of a routed army all the way to the capital had been lost.

On the second day of his ferrying duties the ADC came out to see Phil, who was supervising the cleaning of RN2 lying alongside the jetty. His eau de cologne was less apparent in the open air.

'Change of plan, Gunn,' he said crisply. 'You are to fuel, store up and proceed down to Amara. Collect as many *bellums* as you can and tow them back up here. Go to the Amara quartermaster's store when you get there and give him this authorization chit from me. Instead of your services we find we need a bridge across the river here so we're going to have to build a plank bridge supported on *bellums*. You'll probably have to make a couple of trips. Got it?'

'Yes Sir.'

'And get back here as quick as you can.'

'Aye aye Sir,' Phil saluted. The ADC turned on his heels and returned to his office.

'Well that's a turn-up for the books,' Phil muttered to the coxswain. 'Shan't be sorry to see the back of him though.'

'We going down to Amara, Able Seaman Phil?'

'That's right. Raise steam. Take her along to the fuel barge and top up with coal. I'll go with one of your lads to the stores and meet you there.'

Phil passed the rum, which he had been safeguarding, to one of the leading seamen in the horse boats. He and the Indian crew member then set off to the quartermaster's stores to draw the rations.

They rejoined the launch at the fuel barge, carrying food and leading a sheep, which did not know that it was part of the food. Phil bade the horse boats' sailors a temporary farewell and ordered his crew to slip the mooring ropes. He manoeuvred the launch out into the middle of the river, turned her and headed off downstream. The nonplussed-looking sheep had been tethered on the fo'csle with a bowl of water to drink. Phil handed over to the coxswain to steer.

The going was much quicker with the current behind them, but this made controlling the boat more difficult as she tended to be swept at the whim of the river. After a while the coxswain appeared to master it.

Looking out across the desert plain Phil saw Arabs tending crops around some of the small oases that appeared from time to time. Floods of spring and summer off the distant Caucasus Mountains had subsided and the still baking heat was in the annual process of turning a sodden desert into dust. Occasionally there would be a small group of travelling horsemen and he saw a solitary camel and its rider, robes floating down on either side of the animal. It occurred to Phil that, away from the army and armed naval vessels with which he had been travelling, RN2 was now on its own and unprotected. They were well behind the front line, but this was a strange land in which unpredictable things happened. Phil got out the machine gun and a rifle, which were their only weapons, checked they were in working order and made sure supplies of ammunition were close at hand.

He was still recovering from the aftermath of having to remain on duty for days on end, sounding the depth upriver ahead of the expedition. Once he was satisfied that the coxswain was coping and sticking to the middle of what was now a relatively wide river, Phil went to 'get his head down'.

They were going to need to 'bank up' each night owing to the vagaries of the waterway, which made night steaming impractical, so he arranged for the crew to keep watch individually when they were alongside. There were hardly any human beings about by now but anything unusual and they were to wake him. He slept with the loaded guns.

They had unmoored early in the morning of the second day and Phil, having taken a long night watch, was getting some sleep in the cabin once they were well under way downriver. Suddenly he was woken by the sound of rifle fire close at hand and a peculiar movement of the launch. Running out on deck to the accompaniment of another burst of rifle fire from the bank he found the launch careering across the river, heading for nowhere in particular. It appeared that his Indian coxswain and crew, not liking rifle fire from such close quarters, had ducked down out of harm's way, leaving the launch to itself. The steering wheel was idly turning back and forth and the single sounding pole they had been using had been dropped overboard in their panic.

Phil laid into his crew with an infuriated harangue, of which he had not known himself capable. His anger brought them back shamefacedly to their duties but it was too late and they ran onto a sandbank.

By that time, however, they were so far out into the river as to make marksmanship from the shore ineffective and it ceased. Phil made the coxswain and two seamen jump overboard onto the sandbank and rock the vessel from side to side, eventually launching it into deeper water. There were other occasions when stray rifle shots from hostile Arabs came the way of RN2 but the crew did not jib at them again, realizing that these were wild and inaccurate.

Chapter 42

Where is the Medical Back-up?

Phil had to make two trips down to Amara to fetch enough *bellums* for the army's boat bridge and there were no further incidents. Despite having abandoned their posts he liked his coxswain and crew. After all, they were not service personnel but civilians providing a paid service to the Royal Navy, which they did well. Assuming they survived, they would go back to their villages and families in India to till crops or run boats up and down the rivers there: and they were good river seamen.

The incident with the shots from shore did, however, cause him to muse again on one aspect of the campaign. They had a small first aid box on board and occasionally had needed to take sticking plasters out of it to cover a minor wound such as a cut on the hand. Phil found himself wondering, as he had before, what would be the situation if something serious happened to one of his crew or, say, one of the gun crews in the horse boats. There had been an understandable emphasis on filling the paddle steamers with fighting troops rather than support staff but, apart from one or two medical officers, he had not seen anything much in the way of coping with seriously wounded sailors or soldiers.

There probably were, he mused; he just hadn't come across them.

Although a boat bridge was to be built across the Tigris at Kut, Phil and RN2 were still at the disposal of General Townshend. So on their return the launch was again moored near the army's headquarters. He was thus at hand to receive any orders as to where he was to take the general or his staff. Phil found himself having to spend a considerable amount of time in the foyer of the general's office, to which he did not object as it was more comfortable than the launch. He was still in command of this and so had to visit it frequently. The cleanliness of the launch, maintenance of the steam engine and storing by his Indian crew all needed supervision. He hoped he would not have to see too much of the general's ADC, whom he found cold and distant. Occasionally, in the seat available to him outside the office, he would hear snatches of conversation as the next stage of the campaign was planned.

Army Commander Nixon now ordered Major General Townshend to take his forces further up the river Tigris and set up a base at a place called Aziziya, 60 miles above Kut and the same distance below Baghdad. The distances were much greater by river, up which the navy, some of the troops and all the stores had to travel, for the Tigris wound back and forth in great snaking curves across the plain of Lower Mesopotamia. And so the soldiers marched or travelled in the paddle steamers, which were the only large vessels of shallow enough draught to negotiate the variable depth of the river.

Chapter 43

Nixon Wins the Argument for Taking Baghdad

While Townshend had been consolidating at Kut following its capture, General Nixon got the bit between his teeth. On 3 October he telegraphed Austen Chamberlain, Secretary of State for India, stating that his force was strong enough to take Baghdad, and asking for permission to do so.

The Government of India were firmly of the opinion that this could not be safely done without the return from France and the addition to his force of an Indian division of troops. This would amount to perhaps 10,000 more men. They had absolutely forbidden Nixon to advance beyond Kut without this reinforcement. However, on 5 October, Nixon sent another telegram to the Secretary of State, strongly urging the advance upon and destruction of a shaken enemy. He followed this up with a further communication that General Townshend was, by now, already at Aziziya, halfway to Baghdad. This contravened India's instructions to Nixon not to advance beyond Kut.

Austen Chamberlain was in a difficult position. The British and French attempt to attack Turkey at the Dardanelles, and thus knock that nation out of the war at an early stage, was proving a disaster and the political effect of the capture of Baghdad would offset this. He telegraphed to Nixon and the viceroy that the Cabinet were so impressed by the political and military advantages to be obtained by the occupation of Baghdad that they would make every effort to supply the necessary force. Would one division suffice?

This now put the viceroy in a difficult position. General Nixon was at the head of a victorious army that had fought and won a series of successful engagements. Under him Major General Townshend had acquired a reputation for being invincible. The capture of Baghdad would more than compensate for the failure at the Dardanelles and maintain British prestige throughout the Middle East and India. In the circumstances, Hardinge felt he could not override HM Government in London, which was being advised by the army commander in the field.

Chapter 44

Townshend Points out Baghdad Risks

There came a general order to advance. Phil and his Indian crew lashed the horse boats alongside and followed the steamers. There was no action along the way as the Turks had retreated and set up a strong entrenchment at a place called Ctesiphon, 20 miles below Baghdad. The British disembarked and camped a similar 20 miles below Ctesiphon, at Aziziya. It was now rumoured strongly among the force that the plan was to capture Baghdad, but nobody seemed quite sure.

Military headquarters was now a tented complex close to the river and Phil's launch was still at the general's disposal when not advancing with the horse boats. On one occasion he was seated on the chair provided for him outside General Townshend's office. Through the walls of the tent he could not help overhearing snatches of the general dictating a telegram to his clerk.

Take this for General Sir John Nixon. ' ... the Turkish force is established in position at Ctesiphon ... they have also probably been reinforced from Baghdad. ... If I may be allowed to express an opinion I should say that our object up to the battle of Kut has been the consolidation of the Basra *vilayet** and occupation of the strategic position of Kut ... there is doubt about the Dardanelles situation and consequently the possibility of any small force we may put into Baghdad being driven out again by superior forces from Anatolia ... obliged to retreat along an extremely long line of communications infested by semi-hostile, and on news of our retreat, actively hostile Arabs, then we should on all military grounds occupy ourselves with consolidating our position at Kut. If Government desires to occupy Baghdad ... a methodical advance from

---

* *Mesopotamia was split into the three* vilayets *of Baghdad, Mosul and Basra, which was the most south-easterly of them and with a sea coast.*

Kut by road of two divisions is absolutely necessary unless great risk is to be incurred. It is absolutely impossible to send laden ships upriver now.'

Townshend's dictation was interrupted by the arrival of someone Phil recognized as Major General Delamain. It was he who had commanded the major part of the force that had won the well-planned battle of Kut, which was, nevertheless, fought in extremely difficult conditions. An orderly took him into Townshend's office, now in a headquarters tent. Phil did not hear all of the conversation but Delamain's clipped tones were clear:

My Indian troops are not what they were before the battle of Kut al Amara. When I assaulted the … trenches there some of my Indian troops were without spirit … I am convinced that if they had to assault solidly held trenches, again my troops would not succeed. They are worn out and need rest. They know that Aziziya to the sea is over 300 miles and are beginning to wonder what is to be the end of it all.

Later, a clerk walked past Phil into the general's office and read out Nixon's reply to Townshend's telegram that had suggested the IEF should hang onto Kut rather than attempt to advance further with inadequate numbers. The Turks at Ctesiphon, maintained Nixon, were less in numbers than those Townshend had defeated at Kut. Their morale was low and it was Nixon's intention that we should go for Baghdad as another division of some 10,000 men was on its way from France.

Chapter 45

Memories of Street Games

Back at the launch, having eaten his evening meal, Phil took out the pipe that Petty Officer Bryce had taught him to smoke, lit it and settled down on the stern of the launch to contemplate his situation. He drew on the pipe and his mind went back to life at Teddington in South West London, and an incident that had subsequently caused him to suffer nightmares as a boy.

Living in the same road as Phil and some of his friends had been an elderly lady whose upper lip was well covered with short hairs. 'Hirsute', somebody had described her, but he didn't know what that meant. As 7-year-olds they would taunt her, making sure they were well out of range of the sharp point of the umbrella she wielded in both fine and rainy weather. 'Old Mrs Whiskers,' they would shout at her, fleeing along the pavement until they found their front doors and dashed inside for safety. She was not popular in the street among her own generation and so they did not fear her knocking on doors and complaining to parents. On one such occasion, Phil and his fellows having shouted their taunts were retreating when Phil found that his front door would not open. Perhaps it was bolted from the inside. He was trapped, unable to escape as Old Mrs Whiskers bore down on him. Although he did just open it in time to escape her wrath, the sensation of being trapped became a phobia of his and he subsequently spent many a sleepless night because of it.

Having overheard recent conversations from outside General Townshend's office he found himself feeling similarly trapped. If the people at the top could not agree about the way to proceed, thought Phil, this didn't seem good for lowly soldiers or seamen like himself. There was nothing he could do about it, however, and Phil forced his thoughts to drift back to happier days at Teddington.

Another trick he remembered was that he and his fellows would tie all the door knockers together with a very long piece of string, and then pull the string to set the knockers knocking and run round the corner out of sight. All the inhabitants of the street would come to their doors simultaneously to see who was knocking, causing much merriment among Phil and his friends.

There were the street games. One in the summer when cherries were for sale in Kingston market was 'Cherryog up the Spout'. The boys would eat their cherries but save the stones. They would foregather in the street and find a convenient vertical drainpipe that carried the rain down off the roof and turned at 45° out towards the edge of the pavement. Placing a cherrystone in the palm of their hand, they would bang the palm against the open end of the pipe, firing the stone up as far as possible. It would then run down again and out onto the pavement. He whose cherrystone went farthest was the winner.

Phil, having banished his memories of feeling trapped, smiled at the memory of what now appeared to be such happy days. He wondered where those childhood friends were now that Britain was at war.

Chapter 46

A Bullet in his Pillow

Major General Townshend considered that a grave risk was being run in continuing this advance to Baghdad with only his division of some 9,000 fighting troops, weakened by their nevertheless successful taking of Kut. He thought that the Turks would undoubtedly reinforce Baghdad. They might well have plenty of forces with which to do this as things were clearly not going well for the British in the Dardanelles.

He was a subordinate commander to Nixon and felt it right to give his opinion to the army commander, which he had done. He now thought further argument useless as Nixon evidently considered the British force sufficient and meant to disregard the warning. Townshend also doubted that the promised Indian troops from France would arrive in time. However, his duty was to obey his superior and he would now formulate his plan of battle and submit it accordingly.

* * *

Townshend's ADC emerged from the general's office late one day and addressed Phil. 'We shan't need you any more, Gunn, and the navy say they want you back for the forthcoming advance, so you had better get back to your launch,' he said curtly without looking up from the papers he was carrying.

'Aye aye Sir,' replied Phil. He stood up, put his cap on, saluted and walked out of the door of the tent that constituted military headquarters.

RN2 was berthed against a low jetty by the side of the river and he was as glad to be back in the familiar environment as the Indian crew similarly appeared to be to see him return. Somehow, despite his youth and humble status, the impression they gave was that he represented security to them. Phil checked the vessel and all appeared to be in order. They turned in.

The following morning at about 6.00 am, when they were having a cup of tea, Lieutenant Johnston, the FOO, walked up to the boat.

'Morning, Gunn. We're about to advance and attack the next place up the river, Kutuniya – it's only a few miles. Get underway at 0800 hours and stand by to take your two horse boats with the army as it moves forward. I'll come with you.'

At about five minutes to eight, Johnston returned and jumped aboard as the engines throbbed into action, and Phil supervised the crew in coming alongside one horse boat after another before gently proceeding upstream. On the bank to the right of them he could see the infantry advancing in columns but they soon faded from sight as the river turned away from the primitive road on which they were marching.

Although it was mid-October 1915, the weather was still very hot by day and so both the army and the navy ceased activity when the sun was high to wait for the cooler evening air. Halfway to Kutuniya, Johnston accordingly ordered the launches with their horse boats into the bank to rest up through the hottest hours. The Indian crew put out their bedding in the forecastle and Phil on the launch's upper deck to catch up with sleep in the stifling heat. In the horse boats the seamen gunners also turned in.

Phil did not know how long he had been asleep when the sound of gunfire from not too far away woke him up. It was accompanied by splashes of shells in the water near the launch. He rolled up his bedding rapidly, stowing it away to prepare for action.

The horse boat crews cleared their guns for action, the seamen gunners replying under the guidance of Lieutenant Johnston. He obviously controlled the direction of their fire with a counter-bombardment that drove off some Turkish field artillery that had surprised them. The excitement ended. They had sustained no discernible damage.

That night when laying out his bedding Phil noticed a hole in the pillow that had not been there before. Rummaging around inside it he pulled out a round shrapnel ball (see illustration) that could only have penetrated when the enemy's fusillade came over that afternoon. That could have been in his head rather than the pillow, he mused thoughtfully. Again he pondered on the apparent lack of medical services that the Indian Expeditionary Force had up the Tigris.

Chapter 47

The Fighting Becomes Intense

M orale was high both in the IEF and among the politicians in London. On 2 November 1915, Prime Minister Asquith told the House of Commons:

General Nixon's force is now within measurable distance of Baghdad. I do not think that in the whole war there has been a series of operations more carefully contrived, more brilliantly conducted, and with a better prospect of final success.

Reconnaissance by the cavalry reported that the Turks had pushed a large number of troops downstream from Ctesiphon to a position about 15 miles ahead of the British. Friendly Arabs reported to General Townshend that they were planning to attack his force. The Turks had clearly recovered from their defeat at Kut al Amara.

Townshend consolidated his forces and, although he was hampered by lack of both river and land transport, called up what reinforcements he could. The winding course of the Tigris meant that travelling by boat involved twice the distance on land; yet the river provided the water that was vital to the expedition's progress.

Over the next days few the cavalry out in front was in contact with Turkish troops a number of times and many skirmishes took place. The previous situation with the British force in the ascendant was no longer as clear-cut as it had been and so the attitude of the local Arabs became increasingly hostile. Phil recalled the words of the sophisticated Arab in the market at Basra:

The people here just want to be left alone. We expect you will be the same as the Turks. If we have to take sides we join the side that is winning. We fight against the side that is losing. And we make as much as we can from whoever interferes with us.

RN2, with its horse boats, proceeded upriver in line with the advancing army. The fighting was becoming intense. For longer runs upriver one of the navy's more powerful armed paddle wheelers would tow the horse boats. However, on contact with the enemy, which happened regularly, Phil would retrieve and take them into the riverbank, where they could tie up. Then he would lay out their anchors into the stream to steady them for the accuracy of the seamen gunners. The army's Lieutenant Johnston directed them as before. As the advancing soldiers provided protection against possible Turkish infantry attack on the launch and horse boats, they were not likely to be captured. However, they were frequently the target for artillery attacks as they were clearly causing the Turks considerable damage.

When under way, Arab snipers, paid by the Turks to do so, shot at them rather inaccurately. The seamen gunners on the horse boats retaliated. Fortunately, no one on either launch or horse boat was hit during the advance.

The Turks gradually retired to their well-prepared defensive positions at Ctesiphon. This had been the capital of various ancient civilizations, the only remnant of which was the magnificent brick-built Arch of Ctesiphon, built in the sixth century AD and standing 85 feet up into the sky. But the advancing British and Indian troops had little time to dwell on such archaeological gems.

Chapter 48

The Battle of Ctesiphon

The Turkish position at Ctesiphon consisted of two lines of trenches, the second being 1,200 yards behind the first. These extended out on each side of the river but mostly to the right of the river seen from the British front. This was the obvious side from which an approaching army would advance on Baghdad, 18 miles beyond.

Major General Townshend prepared his plan of attack. He had a total of 13,500 soldiers, but of them only 8,600 were infantry. It was on these, British, Indian and Gurkha troops, that he relied principally to win the battle. He laid his plans with doubt in his mind as to whether defeating the Turks at Ctesiphon was feasible but he had been ordered to do it by his army commander. It was important that he did not convey his doubts to those who would fight the battle.

Townshend divided his force into four columns that would attack different parts of the Turkish trenches, but only on the right-hand side of the river as seen from the British front. The attack would be at different times after dawn according to a prearranged plan. He needed the naval flotilla, consisting of a number of gunboats as well as the launches and their horse boats, to advance and hammer the Turkish trenches with their relatively heavy guns from the river. In preparation for this they moved up, some anchored and others moored against its banks. The Royal Navy's role was to direct its fire against the nearest half of the Turkish front line and it was they who opened the battle.

But they had a problem that General Townshend had clearly not foreseen.

All Townshend's forces were concentrated on the right side of the river, which allowed the Turks unhindered freedom to mount considerable heavy artillery fire against the naval flotilla from the left. The Turkish artillery was well dug in and could have been silenced if British infantry had been

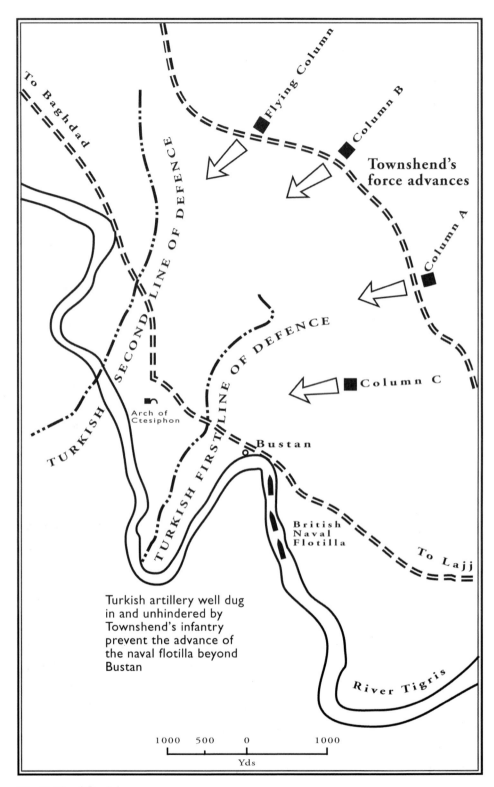

To Baghdad

Flying Column

Column B

Townshend's
force advances

TURKISH SECOND LINE OF DEFENCE

Column A

Arch of
Ctesiphon

TURKISH FIRST LINE OF DEFENCE

Column C

TURKISH

Bustan

British
Naval
Flotilla

To Lajj

Turkish artillery well dug
in and unhindered by
Townshend's infantry
prevent the advance of
the naval flotilla beyond
Bustan

River Tigris

1000   500   0   1000

Yds

The Battle of Ctesiphon.

used against it in co-operation with the navy. But there was no infantry on the left side.

So a frustrated Royal Navy, operating in small river craft, was unable to steam forward against this hail of fire and its supporting gunfire was less effective than had been planned. They were confined to long-range shelling without being able to add the effective close range fire the navy had provided to such good effect at Kut al Amara and in other previous actions.

The riverbanks were about 15 feet high at this point, which made aiming over them difficult even with a forward observing officer to direct. The tall masts of the larger boats also gave the Turkish gunners an aiming point as these were visible over the high banks. Fortunately, RN2 and the horse boats had relatively low profiles and were not such a good target.

From a position lower down the river than they would have liked, the Royal Navy's bombardment started and Phil found himself quickly affected by the 'fog of war' – the chaos that envelopes naval and military forces in action, particularly when schemes do not go quite according to plan. Feeling a little dizzy he worked hard at getting his Indian crew to manoeuvre the launch frequently so as to move the horse boats into positions required by the observing officer. The gun crews in the boats loaded, elevated, trained and fired their 4.7-inch guns as ordered, sweat pouring off them in the warm Mesopotamian day that would turn ice cold at night.

News came via the observing officer that Leading Seaman Thompson, in command of the other launch, RN1, had been hit in the shoulder by a dumdum bullet and had had to be landed. Phil knew that these soft-nosed missiles opened up inside people to make a greater wound, and winced at the thought. There was no news as to who had taken over RN1 to manoeuvre its two horse boats, as Phil was doing.

One of Phil's boats was hit by a Turkish shell but fortunately well above the waterline and without wounding any of its seamen gun crew or igniting the ammunition on board. Splashes arose all around RN2 and the horse boats as Turkish gunners targeted them with increasing accuracy. Other gunboats with taller masts absorbed a number of hits.

And then all went blank.

Chapter 49

Phil is Carried Ashore

Seamen from one of the horse boats carried Phil Gunn's body ashore (see illustration), dressed as it was in white shirt, shorts and gym shoes, and laid it on a bank. There was no time for them to do anything other than put it in the shade of a palm tree during a lull in the action.

The army's column nearest the river advanced on the enemy, vigorously aided, to the best of their reduced ability, by the Royal Navy's bombardment of the Turkish trenches in front of them. In the far distance a further two columns swept in on the Turkish left. This was known as a 'turning attack', with a view to catching them unawares from the side. It was also planned to cut off their line of retreat.

Having distracted the enemy with these attacks on the extremities of their lines, the fourth column pressed forward in the centre to strike at what Townshend considered would be the most vulnerable point of the Turkish front line. He had taken care to radiate a spirit of cheerful optimism in anticipation of the battle. Morale was high in the British forces, with confidence that they would win. However, the general had no doubt that what they were undertaking was a risky enterprise with insufficient forces. All his study of war indicated possible disaster, but he was obliged to carry out the orders of General Nixon, his army commander.

The Turkish vulnerable point was captured after fierce fighting but the turning attack of the two columns on the right had been held back by the Turks. The battle raged all day, with the British capturing and occupying the Turkish first-line trenches before nightfall. They stayed in them all night, the Turks having retreated to their second line.

Townshend, who had ridden across the desert under enemy artillery fire to the position the British had captured, intended to continue the offensive the next day. The trenches in which he and his staff found themselves were full of Turkish and British dead and wounded. Both sides had fought themselves to a standstill.

* * *

The British spent a disturbed night but when daylight broke the next day Townshend was better able to appreciate the condition of his force. Men and animals were exhausted and, being some way from the river, suffering greatly from lack of water. Units had become intermingled and there was much disorganization as a result. Out of a total of 13,500 men, they had lost about one-third dead or wounded. Some who were able to walk wandered about looking for first aid posts but these didn't exist. The severely wounded lay where they fell, hoping that search parties would find them, but it was often hours later if they did.

Vigorous attempts were made to evacuate the wounded but all they had were two-wheeled ox-drawn wooden carts. These un-sprung wagons with iron wheels could only take three or four soldiers, all in acute discomfort as they bumped, some with broken limbs, others with terrible abdominal injuries, over the uneven ground. Men cried out in pain with the lurching of the merciless vehicles and some threw themselves off, unable to bear the agony any longer.

The Turks had lost even more and the two sides licked their wounds and skirmished for two more days before Townshend decided he had to retire downriver to reorganize his force, hopefully incorporating in it the reinforcements that he had been promised.

Chapter 50

The Ox Cart

It was the Indian driver of a passing ox cart that saw the body lying under a palm tree near the spot where British gunboats had been shelling the Turks at the Battle of Ctesiphon. He already had two wounded soldiers in his cart and, like most Indian civilians involved in the Mesopotamia campaign, was both frightened and anxious to get back to his home in the Punjab.

They were now 500 miles from the sea, up a river with an army whose purpose in fighting he did not understand. Accordingly, he resented the authorities whom he held responsible for the army's plight, and the targets for his resentment included the officers, who were merely another form of authority. Furthermore, the attack on Ctesiphon was an attack on what he, a Muslim, considered a holy place. It was the birthplace of Sulman Pak, Mohammed's barber, also considered a holy man. But here was the body of a young sailor who, like himself, had been forced into fighting that now appeared to have no purpose. For a moment he was reminded of his boatman son in the Punjab, back in the village close to the river Jhelum. But this sailor was probably dead. The driver brought his oxen to a halt and eased himself off the draw shaft to go and have a look at the body.

It could not have lain there for very long for no dust had collected on the white seaman's shirt and shorts, just a few stains. He bent over to have a closer look. And then the driver thought he detected a slight movement. He knelt with his ear close to the mouth of the recumbent sailor and felt a faint breath on his ear. He put his hand on the young man's forehead. It was unnaturally hot and his hand became damp with the sweat on the skin.

Was the young sailor irrevocably dying and therefore best left where he lay, or could he be helped to live? If left, the Arabs would strip and murder him anyway.

He made his mind up. The driver was a small man, and it was with difficulty that he hoisted the burly sailor up onto his shoulder and executed a bow-legged running walk over to the ox cart. By stages, he eased the body over the rim of the cart and laid it out as carefully as he could on the floor.

One of the two wounded soldiers groaned at the increased pain the disturbance brought to his injured body, before relapsing back into sleep

The driver lifted Phil Gunn's head up and held a bottle of water to his lips. The liquid ran down his throat and he choked and coughed. Tired eyes opened and stared listlessly ahead before turning to see in whose arms he lay. The eyes closed again and the driver noticed that the skin on the sailor's face and arms was yellow.

* * *

The ox cart was a Red Cross wagon and a medical officer's instructions had been for these to pick up as many wounded as the drivers could take. They should then proceed downriver to Lajj, 7 miles below Ctesiphon, and hand them over to the medical centre there.

They bumped along the uneven track in the light of early morning, Phil lapsing in and out of consciousness. The November sun was gentle as it rose but welcome as the night had been cold. A pair of vultures rose into the air and circled over to the left of the rough track, from which direction Phil could discern faint cries, as could the driver.

'Help me Sir! Don't leave me behind. I am in terrible pain Sir.'

The driver guided the oxen off the track towards the voice, a move that gave even more discomfort to the cart's occupants. An Indian soldier had lain there for an untold period, his wounds untended, longing for death and hoping it would come before marauding Arabs found him. Both his legs were broken and he had several bullet wounds. He was smaller than Phil and the driver had little difficulty in lifting him into the now overloaded wagon. They returned to the uneven track and traversed a large bend in the river that led to Lajj. They saw more bodies that had been stripped and murdered, lacerated by the daggers of the Arabs.

Further on a despairing Indian voice called out of the darkness: 'Margaya Sahib!'… 'dying Sir.' But the driver fixed his eyes on the track ahead and went on. He could do nothing for the dying man as the cart was already overladen. Phil had recovered consciousness enough to hear the pathetic cries and asked the driver where he was. He had little hope that the man would understand his question or that he would comprehend any answer, but fortunately the Indian did know some English, having worked for the army in the Punjab before he came to Mesopotamia. He recounted the circumstances of finding Phil and taking him into the cart. For the rest of the journey Phil was sufficiently conscious to take in what was going on around him.

At times the driver feared for his own safety and that of his charges but the marauders appeared to prefer to work in the concealment of the night. From time to time he would give the half-conscious men water from the bottle. He had filled it up from the river and was painfully aware that its contents were as likely to kill them as the wounds from which his soldiers and one sailor suffered. But it did seem to give them a better chance than death from dehydration.

On Phil there were neither wounds nor signs of blood on the light canvas clothing, just a yellow-skinned face that was very hot, and the driver knew what that meant. As an Indian from the Punjab, his body was relatively resistant to the mosquito bites that often brought white men down. But this young sailor, in from the clean air of the sea, was vulnerable and had obviously suffered a severe attack of malaria fever. He had seen it before in British people in India but they usually had a hospital and professional nursing close at hand. There was no hospital 500 miles up the river Tigris.

Chapter 51

The Medics are Overwhelmed

As they approached Lajj the driver looked around him and saw other springless wagons converging on the tented medical centre. Doubtless they carried similar wounded charges suffering varying degrees of pain. Cries of agony floated across the morning air as the maimed men were bumped over the uneven ground. Such cries struck horror into those less badly hurt but sufficiently conscious to detect the distress around them.

There were also soldiers in ragged uniforms walking, limping and sometimes crawling towards the tents. Some were bandaged and some not. Many had been without water for a day and all were cold from the night they had spent in the open. These were the ones that had survived the ordeal and some wished they had not.

A medical orderly, obviously fatigued and sweat-stained himself, motioned the driver into a queue of carts that slowly progressed towards the nearest tent. Here there would be medical officers to tend the wounded, relieve their pain and, hopefully, start their recovery. An hour went by, and then another.

As they waited Phil recovered consciousness sufficiently to ask the driver what was going on. The driver recounted the events that had occurred since he had found Phil's body under the palm tree at Ctesiphon.

In due course, a harassed-looking medical officer, with sleeves rolled up, emerged from the tent and surveyed the line of ox-drawn carts. Resignation was written on his face as he took off a uniform cap and scratched his head. Another joined him for a brief respite.

'I'd like to know who was responsible for this shambles,' Phil heard one say to the other looking at the pitifully small medical centre the authorities had set up. 'How the hell do they expect a small team like ours to cope with these numbers?'

'You wouldn't believe it but the plan was for the walking wounded to walk forward into Baghdad once we'd captured it!' was the reply. They turned back to their work.

Through the entrance to the tent Phil could see that it was full of mangled humanity. The few medical officers were obviously fully stretched in operating on them, some using techniques in which they had not been trained, it emerged afterwards. They were just doing their best.

But there was no room for another patient in either that tent or the other two close by.

A medical officer came down the line towards the cart in which Phil lay. He stopped at three carts ahead, held out his right arm to indicate a dividing point and called out: 'All carts from here back – go to the riverbank. There is a steamer there. Embark your wounded on that and they will be taken downriver.'

There was a general murmuring from the drivers, who then whipped their oxen, and in some cases mules, out of the line and to the right towards the riverbank. Further progress was initially over rough ground as they moved out of the track. That again elicited groans from the wounded but the surface gradually improved towards the water's edge. Sure enough, a small paddle steamer was alongside, and up a wooden gangplank about a hundred wounded men were slowly embarked. Some were carried, others walked, and a few crawled.

Phil, still lapsing in and out of consciousness, was among those who were carried. Two medical orderlies lifted him from the cart onto a stretcher, bore him up the gangplank and across to a position on the upper deck away from the shore. They lifted him from the stretcher, laid him down on the deck and returned for more. He didn't get a mattress. There were only enough of these for the most severely wounded.

Chapter 52

The River Journey Through Hell

The paddle steamer had previously been used for transporting mules and cavalry horses upriver. There had been no time to scrub the inevitable excreta from the decks. The casualties lay among this, some sickened by it and vomiting. The unconscious were preserved from such suffering but not from the infections they were unwittingly absorbing.

The process of embarking the wounded took much of the day and went on until there was no further space left in the steamer.

Although late in the year, with the Tigris flowing gently, it was too late to negotiate the ever-changing channels at night. The steamer remained alongside until the next dawn made safer navigation feasible. Then she nosed out into the river to negotiate the 100-mile voyage to Kut. There were only sips of water for the wounded, for there was no food.

Steady rain didn't seem to fall in Mesopotamia. There were only sudden, violent storms. That night, with the steamer banked up alongside to await another dawn, the first of these descended on the wounded. Strong winds swept the rain in under the canvas awnings, whose normal role was to protect those on deck from a fierce sun. Such bedding as there was, and Phil had none, became swiftly soaked. In his half-conscious state he sensed rather than saw the pounding of the heavy water droplets. The wounded lay there in their soaked dejection. For some who had reached the brink it was too much and they degenerated into a welcome death.

The following day they reached Kut, where some of the sick and wounded were transferred to other ships to relieve the overcrowding. There was now some food and water. They were still packed in alongside each other, with little space to move and none in which to relieve themselves. Some were unconscious, others in agony from gunshot or shell wounds, some near to death, as this convoy of despair started to undergo the further 290-mile journey downriver.

The few doctors did their best. With limited bandages and medicine they aimed to dress wounds every two days, inadequate though this was. Some did not have their wounds looked at between leaving the battlefield and death. The voyage was delayed as the ships ran aground in the shallow, poorly charted Tigris. On one such occasion the sound of rifle fire close by penetrated Phil's unconscious state and he half opened his eyes to see flashes on the nearby shore. Aground and stationary, they were being attacked by Arabs from the banks. A body near him shuddered and was still. Twice the convoy of wounded had to return to Kut.

Food and properly filtered drinking water again ran out and only limited replenishment of these vital supplies was possible.

It was now nearly a fortnight since most of them had either fallen sick or been wounded. The too few medical staff deliberated as to whether they should push the bodies of the dead overboard in order to give a greater chance of survival to those still alive. They decided not, but carried the corpses to an area set aside for the dead, first removing the living still lying in it.

Chapter 53

Phil Moves Towards Death

Phil Gunn drifted in and out of consciousness, gradually getting weaker, not from battle wounds but malarial fever combined with lack of food. He had succumbed as a result of long exposure to the vicious bites of the Mesopotamia river mosquitoes sucking blood from their victims, and now lay among the wounded in the *Mejidieh*, a paddle steamer temporarily converted to a hospital ship. Sometimes he felt overpoweringly hot and would be covered in perspiration but this could suddenly change to an extreme chill. Around him people were dying. From time to time a bottle of water was held to his lips. Men were too weak to get to the very few lavatories in the ship and relieved themselves where they lay or stood. Dysentery broke out among them.

* * *

Major Carter of the Indian Medical Service stood on the deck of the hospital ship *Varela* at Basra, waiting for the wounded from the Battle of Ctesiphon. He subsequently described the scene:

> I was standing on the bridge in the evening when the *Mejidieh* arrived. I saw that she was absolutely packed with over 600 men and had been for twelve days. When she was about 300 or 400 yards off it looked as if she was festooned with ropes. The stench when she was close was quite definite, and I found that what I mistook for ropes were dried stalactites of human faeces. The patients were so huddled and crowded together that they could not perform the offices of nature clear of the edge of the ship, and the whole of the ship's side was covered with human faeces. A certain number of men were standing and kneeling on the immediate perimeter of the ship. Then we found a mass of men huddled up anyhow – some with blankets and some without. They were lying in a pool of

dysentery and dejecta generally from head to foot. With regard to the first man I examined, I put my hand into his trousers and I thought that he had a haemorrhage. His trousers were full almost to his waist with something warm and slimy. I took my hand out. It was dysentery. The man had a fractured thigh and this was perforated in five or six places. He had apparently been writhing about the deck of the ship. Some men, both Indian and British, had limbs splinted with wood strips from Johnny Walker whisky boxes.

With care, for many of them were now wisps of humanity, the sick and wounded still alive were disembarked from the *Mejidieh* and other vessels and taken to hospital beds that had been prepared for them. There were too many for the actual hospital but other buildings had been commandeered and hastily equipped. The Basra authorities realized they had a gruelling task ahead.

Chapter 54

Besieged in Kut

Major General Townshend had been forced to retreat from the Battle of Ctesiphon, which the British forces had theoretically won. The Turks estimated they had lost 9,500 men against the IEF's 4,000. However, Townshend's casualties were such in relation to the overall size of his force that he decided to retire. They would regroup at Kut al Amara, 90 miles by road but 140 by river down the winding Tigris.

They were pursued by the Turks, who were kept at bay until Townshend and his force, which had made a successful though gruelling retirement to Kut, were safely into it on 3 December 1915. The Royal Navy, in armed but small vessels because of the shallow water, fared relatively less well. Including Phil's launch, RN2, and the horse boats, they fought a vigorous rearguard action in defence of the army against the pursuing Turks. However, the Tigris wound its way tortuously across the plains of Mesopotamia while the route down which the army and its pursuers marched was straight. The navy also had repeatedly to stop and haul off the force's troop-carrying paddle steamers when these grounded in the mud of the shallow Tigris. This inevitably made them targets for Turkish field guns and snipers, who could travel freely over the country whereas their small vessels were restricted to the river. A number had been sunk or captured.

The Turks had not had it all their own way. On one occasion the navy discovered at dawn that a large body of Turkish troops had advanced in the night and camped quite close by. This gave the naval guns an easy target when daylight revealed their presence and merciless execution of the Turks resulted, but the navy suffered severe losses as well. However, it took a little pressure off Townshend's retiring columns on their march back to Kut.

At Kut the army was surrounded by Turkish forces but nobody doubted that a powerful relief force would be gathered and the siege raised within a short space of time. The wounded had been sent down by river to Basra

* * *

On 4 December 1915, the Secretary of State for India, in London, Mr Austen Chamberlain, concerned that drama was unfolding in Mesopotamia, telegraphed the army commander:

> On arrival wounded at Basra. Please telegraph urgently particulars and progress.

Nixon replied:

> Wounded satisfactorily disposed of. Many likely to recover in country comfortably placed in hospitals at Amara and Basra. General condition of wounded very satisfactory. Medical arrangements under circumstances of considerable difficulty working splendidly.

Nixon subsequently denied having drafted this telegram.

Major Carter, of the Indian Medical Service, who had witnessed the arrival of the *Mejidieh* with its appalling cargo of sick, wounded, those near to death and dead, subsequently complained of the facilities available to him for caring for the wounded. He was treated rudely by the force's senior medical officer, Surgeon General Hathaway, and threatened with arrest and dismissal from his job as 'a meddlesome, interfering faddist'.

Chapter 55

'One Less To Watch Dyin'

Occasionally, in his half-conscious state, Phil was able to take in snatches of conversation.

'That's a sailor, ain't it?' he heard a junior medical orderly commenting on coming across his recumbent body among the filth on *Mejidieh's* upper deck. 'Is 'e alive?'

'Feel 'is pulse,' said his senior orderly.

The junior felt the young man's pulse. 'Yes 'e is – just.'

'Well 'e won't be for much longer unless we gets 'im off of 'ere. Ave a look in 'is pocket. See if we can find out which ship 'e's from.'

The orderly found the sailor's trouser pocket and felt in it, withdrawing a dirty scrap of paper, which he unfolded.

'It's a letter from 'ome. "Dear Phil," it says. "I 'ope you're gettin' on all right in HMS *Clio*. Where is she now?"'

'I can tell you where she is,' exclaimed the senior orderly. 'She's that thing with three masts over there!'

Their gaze went across the river, where the *Clio*, too deep in the water to have gone all the way up the Tigris, lay peacefully alongside.

'Well we'd better get 'im over there. That'll be one less to watch dyin'.'

There were no officers about. The orderlies were stretched in their responsibilities anyhow. But an Arab in his *bellum* was hanging around off the side of the *Mejidieh* in order to make some money when the opportunity arose.

The senior orderly felt in the recumbent Phil's other pocket and withdrew two rupees he found there.

''Ere, Mustafa!' he called. 'Want to earn some fuckn' *baksheesh*?'

'Oh yes, Sahib, me very good boatman service, Sahib.'

The Arab boatman poled over towards the ship, whose sides rose only 2 feet above the water level.

The two orderlies lifted Phil up from the bed of filth in which he lay and over to the *Mejidieh's* side. One clambered down into the canoe-like *bellum*, with its high, pointed rising bow and stern. The Arab steadied the boat alongside, allowing them to pass the body down and lay it on the bottom boards.

'Now listen, mate,' said the senior orderly pointing. 'You takes this sailor over to that ship there. You treats 'im very careful and when you gets alongside you shouts up to 'em that you've got one of theirs to return to 'em. They will send sailors down to carry him up on board. Understand?'

'Oh yes, Sahib. I do all you say werry carefully. How many rupees?'

''Ere's two rupees. Now you sees this rifle? Me and my friend'll be watching you all the way. You gets it wrong and you'll get a bullet up yer backside. Savvy?'

'Indeed, Sahib. I do everything right. No bullet up backside.'

'Off yer goes then.' The senior orderly picked up the rifle to indicate he meant what he said. Phil felt himself being poled by the Arab gently across the Tigris.

Chapter 56

'Alive But That's About All I Can Say'

The crew of HMS *Clio* had mixed feelings. Far from the front because of the draught of their ship, they had heard that the Royal Navy had been somewhat frustrated in its efforts to support the army at Ctesiphon. Townshend's battle plan had, apparently, been to concentrate all his troops on one side of the river. This had allowed the unhindered Turkish artillery, on the other side, to prevent the navy from advancing sufficiently far upriver to provide the powerful gunfire support of which it was capable.

Some of the sailors in the battle, principally those manning the horse boats, had been loaned from the *Clio* and at this stage no one quite knew who had survived and who perished. Tied in with these concerns was the fact that the bulk of *Clio's* sailors would have liked to have been part of the action.

It was late in the forenoon. 'Up spirits' was about to be sounded in *Clio* to call those responsible to draw the rum ration for their mess. This would be followed by 'Cooks to the galley' for collection and setting up of the dinner in each mess.

* * *

Across the Tigris a solitary Arab poled his *bellum* towards the ship. There was nothing unusual about this; the river close to Basra was always the scene of waterborne activity.

In this instance the *bellum* appeared to the officer of the watch on the upper deck to be heading directly towards the ship in a somewhat purposeful manner. He removed the telescope from beneath his arm, raised it and, balancing it expertly between first and second finger of each hand, studied the approaching craft. There appeared to be a body lying on its bottom boards. He re-focussed the lenses of the telescope deftly, the result of long practice.

The body appeared to be dressed in very dirty sailor's white shirt and shorts. It didn't move.

The Arab boatman manoeuvred the *bellum* across the current, deftly turning it up parallel with the *Clio* and sliding it alongside the vertical ladder hanging down the ship's side. The officer of the watch looked down into the boat.

'By God!' he exclaimed. 'It's young Gunn.'

Then, to the boatman, 'Wait alongside!'

Hastily summoning the quartermaster and boatswain's mate, his assistants on the forenoon watch, he urged them down into the *bellum*. They picked up and gently eased Phil, filthy from all he had been through, over the ship's side, laying him gently on the deck. They had known their young fellow seaman had volunteered for 'possibly hazardous duties' and had disappeared on these. They had no idea what happened to him after that.

Meanwhile, the officer of the watch had sent for the ship's surgeon, who arrived a few moments later.

'He looks in a bad way.'

'He is,' replied the surgeon, who had brought his medical bag with him in anticipation. 'I'll examine him here where he lies.' He pulled the shirt up below the armpits, noting how hot the young man's body was. It had obviously perspired greatly but dehydration meant that there was now little moisture left in the emaciated frame. Taking his stethoscope from the bag he put it to his ears, placing the head of the instrument above Phil's heart. They waited for the verdict.

The surgeon moved the stethoscope around on the young man's chest, listening at various points above heart and lungs before removing the instrument from his ears, folding and putting it back into the bag.

'Well, he's alive, but that's just about all I can say. His body is also very hot. Can you get him carried gently down to my sick bay so that I can give him a proper going over? I must get some water into him. What did you say his name was?'

'Gunn – Able Seaman. He joined us as a boy seaman but volunteered to go upriver – a bit before you joined. And this is the result.'

'I'd say he's lucky to be alive looking at his general state and the colour of his skin,' replied the surgeon, running fingers over Phil's forehead. 'Let's get him down below and see if we can keep him that way. Will you let the captain know?'

The ship's sick berth attendant was summoned and arrived with a stretcher. Together he and the boatswain's mate lifted Phil onto it and bore the stretcher slowly back to the ladderway just forward of the ship's wheel and down to the lower deck. Followed by the surgeon they took him aft to the small sick bay on the starboard side and placed him on the bunk in it.

'Better clean him up a bit Sir?' asked the SBA.

'Let's do our best to make sure he lives first,' Phil heard the surgeon reply as they went about their business. Together they raised the young man's head and gently eased some water down his throat. 'He's thin and emaciated. In this condition I might have to feed him through a vein. His body temperature is also dangerously high.'

* * *

And so for two hours they worked on saving Phil's life. The surgeon diagnosed him as suffering from a severe attack of malarial fever, initially caused by repeated mosquito bites but exacerbated by a fortnight of virtual neglect as he had been carried down the Tigris following the battle of Ctesiphon. He gave him an intravenous injection of quinine. They cooled his body with ice. The shallow breathing became more regular.

'That's all we can do for the moment.' The surgeon stood up from his work and looked at the body in front of him. 'Clean him up now, but do it gently. Give him a thorough blanket bath and then get a seaman to help you stretcher him up onto the forecastle. Lay him on a mattress under the awning where he'll be cool, and go on applying ice to his body. I'll have a look at him later.'

Chapter 57

A Conversation with the Captain

It was not until the next morning that Phil found himself in a fully conscious state and first opened his eyes, woken by a cold application of ice to his forehead. At first he had no idea where he was. Then, looking past the hand that was applying the ice, he saw first a canvas awning above his head and then the barrel of a large gun. It gradually dawned on him that he was back lying on the forecastle in his beloved *Clio*, or at least she seemed beloved after what he had been through.

'What's happening?' he asked the sick berth attendant weakly.

'We were quite surprised you're still alive,' was the reply. 'God alone knows what you've been through judging by the state you were in when you got here.'

His cooling work completed for the moment, the SBA looked at Phil.

'Feel like some grub?'

'Not much.'

'You've got to have something. You haven't got any strength but what you have got, we've got to keep up. I'll bring you some bread and butter.' He vanished in the direction of the galley.

Phil turned his gaze up onto the undemanding sight of the canvas awning and tried to collect his thoughts. He remembered taking the launch towing the two horse boats up the river and the tempo of battle increasing. He recalled mooring the boats alongside the riverbank just below Ctesiphon. The 4.7-inch guns in the horse boats, under the instructions of the forward observing officer, bombarded the enemy over the high banks in support of the army. Then his mind went blank.

There was a series of disconnected recollections. He could just remember bumping through the night in a wooden cart over rough ground, distant voices and the cart driver recounting the events of the grim journey to him during a period of consciousness. Then there was lying on the deck of a ship amid filth, recumbent bodies around him and sometimes under heavy rain. He could recall the sound of rifle bullets whistling over him and occasionally a groan as an already wounded man was hit by one. Each recollection was separated by periods of blankness when Phil realized he must have been unconscious.

The SBA returned with some bread and butter and bully beef sandwiches. There had been a lot of bully beef and Phil liked it but he was only able to eat very little before lapsing into sleep.

* * *

That afternoon, HMS *Clio's* captain came, sat down and talked to him.

'Well, *you've* been through it, Gunn. How are you feeling now?'

'A bit stronger Sir.'

'I think we last saw you between Qurna and Amara when you went off in the launches because we couldn't get up any further. Tell me what happened.'

Phil weakly went through the events as he remembered them. The capture of Amara. Having to pole ahead of the army in their transport paddle steamers to keep them in the main channel. The mirages. Manoeuvring the horse boats to bombard the Turks who sniped at them from the banks. Watching the advance of the army as the guns in the horse boats shelled the enemy.

'Did you hear that we lost Lieutenant Commander Cookson?' enquired the captain.

'Yes Sir, I was there. I saw it happen.'

'Were you indeed? He was a sad loss. We miss him a lot.'

'Do you know what happened to Leading Seaman Thompson in RN1 and the Indian crews of the launches Sir? And who took over from me in RN2? And the gun crews of the horse boats?'

'We got a message that your launch and some horse boats got down to Kut al Amara with the army, which is besieged there. The horse boat gun crews were providing gunfire in the defence of Kut. Regrettably, your opposite number, Leading Seaman Thompson of RN1, was hit in the shoulder by a dumdum bullet farther up the Tigris. He was taken ashore to a desert dressing station but sadly they couldn't save him and he died. They appear to be having great trouble with the medical arrangements up there. Then your launch, RN2, was unfortunately hit and sunk by enemy gunfire and all its crew killed (see illustration). I don't know who your relief was or even if one was appointed, but only the fact that you collapsed with severe malarial fever means that you survived and are with us now.'

The captain could see that the young man was not only saddened at these bitter revelations but also tired, and he left him to sleep. As Phil drifted off his mind dwelt on the three who had set out to direct the movements of the launches, horse boats and the guns. Of the three, Cookson, Thompson and himself, only he had survived ... only just.

Chapter 58

The Fate of Townshend's Force

The plan now was to assemble a strong force farther down the Tigris and return to relieve the besieged 13,000 British and Indians at Kut al Amara.

General Nixon, the army commander, fell ill and his place was taken by another general. Large numbers of men were arriving by sea at Basra with the relief of Kut in mind but the transport, by river or land, was inadequate to get them up to the front. Weather conditions turned against the relieving force. The Turks reinforced their troops and entrenched themselves strongly around Kut.

It was never relieved, nor was it captured by the Turks. General Townshend was forced to surrender to them with his men on the point of starvation in April 1916. The surviving British and Indian troops were taken into captivity and marched to Turkey. So were the survivors of the naval gun crews in the horse boats that Phil Gunn had towed and positioned to bombard the enemy. Of 2,500 British servicemen on the march, 1,750 died. Of 9,300 Indians, 2,500 died or disappeared. In its unsuccessful attempts to recapture Kut the relieving force lost a further 23,000 officers and men.

Chapter 59

Recovery

Those in the navy who had survived or escaped capture rejoined their ships. *Clio* left the Persian Gulf for the ship's company to recuperate after a long period in an alien climate. The living conditions of an enclosed ship in the environment of the river Tigris had led to considerable illness. Few needed the rest more than Phil.

The ship sailed to Ceylon (now Sri Lanka), most of them feeling better for the sea winds that swept through the messdecks. In Colombo, half of the ship's company remained on board to carry out repairs and embark fresh stores. The other half, a very weak Phil among them, was dispatched up into the mountains in the centre of the island to a naval rest camp.

As an invalid Phil was accompanied by a sick berth attendant, climbing up into the mountains by train, from which he was able to admire a view of green jungle vegetation and tea estates. It was a refreshing contrast to the heat, flies and mosquitoes of the Mesopotamian desert. Still alternately shivering and sweating from his malarial fever, Phil was put to bed in the camp hospital.

A tropical Christmas was approaching but the air up in the grass-clad hills felt like that of an English spring as he eased himself weakly up to look out of an open window. Flowers were blooming that would be out in an early English summer. Gradually he started to feel better.

Christmas morning came with Phil still lying in bed feeling weak as he recovered from the fever. Dozing quietly, he was awakened from the quiet of the hospital by the sound of voices raised in song. They appeared to be drawing nearer. Then a group of about a dozen of his shipmates entered and came to stand around his bed. They had come to bring young Phil Gunn Christmas greetings accompanied by carols, which they continued to sing as they stood in a semicircle around him.

A lump came into his throat as these tough, burly seamen sang their carols to him. Tears welled up in his eyes. He had never loved sailors as much as he loved them at that moment.

Chapter 60

Farewell to *Clio*

It was not until January 1916 that Phil was strong enough to walk. He was taken out to one of the tea plantations in the surrounding hills and sat on the verandah of the planter's bungalow where, with other guests, he was given cups of tea. Forever after he would compare tea with that which he drank on that occasion. He would visualize not only the taste of the tea but also the scene, the view across the peaceful hills and valleys and the positions on the verandah of the planter and his guests. He found himself the subject of considerable interest among these guests. They were well aware of the Mesopotamia campaign and the world news it was now making.

Gradually Phil recovered his strength and was eventually fit enough to return to HMS *Clio* in Colombo. Here he was told that he had been promoted to leading seaman, the first step up the official ladder of responsibility. In fact, by a quirk of war, the responsibility that had been placed upon him up the river Tigris had far exceeded that normally placed upon this rank.

He was to spend only a few more days in *Clio*. The medical authorities had decided that he should be invalided from the East Indies station because of his malarial condition. He had joined her as a boy seaman. Three and a half years later, he was to leave her as a 20-year-old leading seaman, proudly wearing on his left sleeve the anchor that indicated the rank.

Phil was transferred to another warship for the voyage home and found himself musing upon his lot. He was grateful to his father for encouraging him to go far afield and to tough Petty Officer Jock Bryce for training him so thoroughly in the ways of the sea. Finally, there was the inspiration of his hero, the late Lieutenant Commander Cookson VC, DSO whom he had seen die so gallantly.

Epilogue

From 1914–1916, little information had seemed to leak out of Mesopotamia. As news of the immense suffering and lack of medical resources there became known, a storm of outrage broke in Britain. A commission was set up and blame cast far and wide. Most at fault for the medical failure were the senior medical officers in the IEF and India. Nixon, the 'general in a hurry', had ordered the attack on Baghdad without enough troops, proper transport or medical facilities.

The Turks never threatened the Royal Navy's supply of oil from Southern Persia, the defence of which was the original sole purpose of the campaign. Casualties from the Expeditionary Force to Mesopotamia totalled nearly 100,000, of whom close on one-third were dead, half of those from disease.

In 1917, a far greater number of troops than had been made available to Major General Townshend, again aided by the Royal Navy, drove the Turks back. Kut and Baghdad were captured. Elsewhere in the Middle East, General Allenby fought the Turks northward through Palestine. In this he was assisted by an Arab revolt against them, spurred on by the man later known as Lawrence of Arabia. On 30 October 1918, the Turkish government signed an armistice. The war with the Turks had come to an end.

Phillip Gunn, newly advanced to leading seaman, was awarded the Distinguished Service Medal for his work with the horse boats. He rose to the rank of captain, Royal Navy, serving in and commanding ships between the wars and during the Second World War. In June 1944, it fell to him to tell Winston Churchill that seriously bad weather in the English Channel had improved sufficiently for a seaborne invasion of Europe to go ahead. For the last thirty years of his life he was a landscape artist.

Bibliography

Unpublished Sources
Imperial War Museums
National Army Museum
National Maritime Museum
Notes made by Captain Phillip Gunn, DSM, RN and conversations between him and the
    author over many years
Royal Naval Museum & Library
The Times (online archive)

Published Material (in the possession of the author)
Hansard (relevant sections), UK Parliament, London (1914–1917)
History of the Great War – Medical Services, volume 4 – Mesopotamia, HMSO, London (1924)
Official History of the 1914–1918 War – Mesopotamia Campaign, Vols 1–4, Imperial War
    Museum, London (1925)
The Times and other newspaper archives of the period (relevant sections)

Anglesey, Marquess of, *A History of the British Cavalry 1816–1919*, Vol 6 1914–1918 –
    Mesopotamia, Leo Cooper/Pen & Sword, London (1995)
Barker, A.J., *The Neglected War – Mesopotamia 1914–1918*, Faber & Faber, London (1967)
Baynham, Henry, *Men from the Dreadnoughts*, Hutchinson, London (1976)
Callwell, Maj Gen Sir C.E., *Life of Sir Stanley Maude*, Constable, London (1920)
Candler, Edmund, *The Long Road to Baghdad* Vols 1 & 2, Cassell, London (1919)
Cato, Conrad, *The Navy in Mesopotamia 1914–1917*, Constable, London (1917)
Dorsetshire Regiment, History of – 1914–1919, Vols 1 & 2, Henry Ling, Dorchester (1932)
Farwell, Byron, *Armies of the Raj 1858–1947*, W.W. Norton, New York & London (1989)
Gilmour, David, *Curzon*, John Murray, London (1994)
Hall, Lt Col L.J., *Inland Water Transport in Mesopotamia*, Constable, London (1921)
Hardinge, Lord, *My Indian Years 1910–1916*, John Murray, London (1948)
Harvey, Lt Cdr W.B., *Downstairs in the Royal Navy*, Brown, Son & Ferguson, Glasgow (1979)
Howell, Georgina, *Daughter of the Desert, Gertrude Bell*, Macmillan, London (2006)
Hoyt, Edwin P., *The Last Cruise of the Emden*, Andre Deutsch, London (1967)
James, Lawrence, *Raj – The Making of British India*, Little, Brown, London (1997)
Keegan, John, *The First World War*, Hutchinson, London (1998)
Lance, David, 'Meals on the Mess Deck', article in *History Today*, London (July 1978)
Lawrence, T.E., *Seven Pillars of Wisdom*, Jonathan Cape, London (1935)
Leland, Lt Col F.W., *With the M.T. in Mesopotamia*, Naval & Military Press, Sussex (2004)

Marshall, Lt Gen Sir William, *Memories of Four Fronts*, Ernest Benn, London (1929)

Maxwell, Gavin, *A Reed Shaken by the Wind*, Longmans, London (1957)

McKee, C., *Sober Men and True – Sailors' Lives in the Royal Navy 1900–1945*, Harvard University Press, Massachusetts (2002)

Mousley, Capt E.O., *The Secrets of a Kuttite*, John Lane, London (1921)

Murphy, Lt Col C.C.R., *Soldiers of the Prophet*, Naval & Military Press, Sussex (originally 1921)

Nash, N.S., *Chitral Charlie*, Pen & Sword, Barnsley (2010)

Nunn, VAdm Wilfred, *Tigris Gunboats – 1914–1917*, Andrew Melrose, London (1932)

Snelling, Stephen, *The Naval VCs of the First World War*, Sutton Publishing, Stroud (2002)

Spackman, Col W.C., *Captured at Kut – Prisoner of the Turks*, Pen & Sword, Barnsley (2008)

Thesiger, Wilfred, *The Marsh Arabs*, Longmans Green, London (1964)

Townshend, Charles, *When God Made Hell*, Faber & Faber, London (2010)

Townshend, Maj Gen Sir Charles, *My Campaign in Mesopotamia*, Thornton Butterworth, London (1920)

Trystan Edwards, A., *British Bluejacket 1915–1940*, Simpkin Marshall, London (1940)

Turkish Army, Notes on the, 1915, Naval & Military Press, Sussex (originally 1915)

Von Sanders, Liman, *Five Years in Turkey*, US Naval Institute, Annapolis USA (1927)

Wells, Captain John, *The Royal Navy, an illustrated social history 1870–1982*, Sutton Publishing, Stroud (1994)

Wilcox, Ron, *Battles on the Tigris*, Pen & Sword, Barnsley (2006)

Wilson, Sir Arnold, *Loyalties: Mesopotamia 1914–1917*, Oxford University Press, London (1930)

Yeats-Brown, F, *Bengal Lancer*, Gollancz, London (1930)

Index